W9-BUN-039

Blackness
and
the Adventure
of
Western Culture

BLACKNESS

AND

THE ADVENTURE

OF

WESTERN CULTURE

by

GEORGE E. KENT

Library, MC
Champaign Centennial High School
Champaign, Illinois

THIRD WORLD PRESS, CHICAGO, ILLINOIS 60619

Copyright © 1972 by George Kent

All rights reserved. No part of this book may be reproduced, stored in
retrieval systems, or transmitted in any form, by any means, including
mechanical, electronic, photocopying, recording, or otherwise without
prior written permission of the publisher.

First Edition
Third Printing
ISBN: 0-88378-026-7

Third World Press
7524 S. Cottage Grove Ave.
Chicago, IL 60619

Cover concept, illustration and design
by Wyatt Hicks

Manufactured in the United States of America

FOR
MY WIFE—DESIRE
MY CHILDREN—EDWARD AND SHERALD
MY MOTHER AND FATHER, MRS. LOUISE
AND MR. IRBY D.
AND
FOR THE BLACK STUDENT

Library I M C
Champaign Centennial High School
Champaign, Illinois

Contents

Introduction

"Sit where the light corrupts your face,
Mies Vanderohe retires from grace
And the fair fables fall. . ."
—Gwendolyn Brooks, *In the Mecca*

I BEGAN WRITING THIS INTRODUCTION BY TRYING TO say something of conscious intentions, and of my hope that, if I had successfully fulfilled them, they would be useful in effecting some shift in the criticism of black literature. But a voice blocked me and my writing. It kept saying: George, You're lying, man. It's not that your essays appeared, in several instances, over a period of years. The problem is that you must say, "I tried to do this and that or to avoid doing this and that." And that way you are double trapped: by a rhetoric that falsifies and confuses conscious striving and achieved unselfconscious rhythms. So say things that you're really clear about, and can express simply and clearly.

Well, all right! I mean—mostly.

Let's put it this way. The reader, I hope, will find no *rigid* allegiance to traditional high ground humanism. By high ground humanism, I mean the established values implicit in white writers (whether agonized over or promoted), derived from Hebrew, Greek, and Roman traditions: the assumed triumph of the individual, the clarity of truth, the existence of transcendental beauty, the shining virtues of rationality, the glory of democratic freedom, and the range of Christian and Platonic assumptions that tend to form stubborn threads in the warp and woof of white tradition as a systematic and *abstract* universalism.

9

What I'm saying is that the writer is permitted to step where-ever he wills, and, as humble critic, my job is to hang loose and follow. Which means that I'll follow him into high humanistic ground, if that's where he leads, and stand by holding a flashlight to see what rhythms he can make visible and throbbing. And I'll stand with him in the cool thickets in the low grounds of lonesome valleys where things go down dense and all definitions dissolve as they resolve or hold themselves together by dint of home made existence-ism clubs.

I—outsider-insider, insider-outsider—follow.

But no rigid pledge of allegiance to the traditional humanistic high ground which, at best, becomes a refuge for Blacks only when we infuse it with our own triumphant rhythms—as say was done with Christianity by Black religion and Black folkloric forms. Other wise, traditional high ground humanism threatens to crumble at the approach of simple fact (the millions of Blacks dumped into the sea or torched out of existence or ground up by various devices as they were being "redeemed" by the white cultivators of the ground; or the whip-crack of plantation boss's voice down home; or the stab of the policeman's light in your rear-view mirror; or at the muffled tick of the computer in this machine culture.

So I'm listening for the voices of ancestors to enrich the reson-ance of contemporary black men. Voices sometimes cynical: sharp-edged. Ellison's Invisible narrator's grandfather's voice. Or some old black farmer who described that man a black stranger was about to sharecrop with: "X is a good man—as far as white folks go." Meaning, don't be no fool now; X fulfills a contract, but still, at certain points, his whiteness overtakes him. Or a certain noted ball-player saying, "Don't look back, something might be gaining on you." Or that sign, still present but simply less visible, saying, "Nig-ger, read and run! If you can't read, run!" Or perhaps just a line from a song: "If *trouble* don't get you, *time* will take you out." Well—work it on out.

In sum, definitions provided by folk and cultural tradition, loose-ly defined, on which the writer can enforce as much signification as the definitions can be made to bear. For the black writer has by no means massively absorbed his folk and cultural traditions and forms, as evidenced by the little use to which the folk sermon and the supernatural and conjure traditions are put. These traditions offer,

10

of course, a resource—not a prison. They are convenient passports to a Blackness beyond simple sloganeering and rhetorical assertion.

Now there are terms that today are sterile categories or shifters of the nature of reality at the very moment they attempt to make coherent statements: *protest,* meaning really tract or special pleading; *transcending* (the narrow and parochial concerns of the black experience and thus arising to the level of Man); *universalism,* meaning usually a validation of Western high ground versions of universalism. Today these terms have revealed themselves as game names. For example, the term *protest* covered Richard Wright for thirty years, concealed his depths from us, so that we are just now beginning to find out what his meaning for us is. *Transcending* becomes all too quickly reducing the tensions of the black experience; become faceless. And the problem with *universalism* is that its current use misdirects the writer and the critic, leads to vague abstractions (Man, the Human Condition), and packs concealed cultural referents. Any universalism worthy of recognition derives from its depths of exploration of the density, complexity, and variety of a people's experience—or a person's. It is achieved by going down deep—not by transcending.

Often, *universalism,* to the degree that it is being genuinely recognized, is simply an acknowledgment that "others" now have achieved the psychological readiness necessary for entrance into the work. Thus people who would earlier have called Wright's fiction simply "protest," are now beginning to see him as "universal." The *blues,* which at one time was a form completely addressed to Blacks and, when recognized at all, were seen largely as something quaint, are now universal. This fact indicates that an America *now* exists which is upset over the issue of deep communication with the self, an issue not easily escapable in black culture which the blues made a career of dealing with ages ago. Changes in psychological readiness have had a good deal to do with periods of sudden intensity of focus upon such writers as Hawthorne and Melville and the growth of acceptance of Yiddish heroes and literature. Thus any real concept of universality poses questions both for audience and for writer. Let me admit that I was not sufficiently wary about such matters when I wrote the essay on Baldwin.

Equally foolish, it seems to me, is the energy wasted upon whether one is to be a black writer or *writer* (who happens to be black). The issue would hardly be worth discussing, if some important black writers had not, to their hurt, taken it so seriously as to diminish their creative powers. Now the simple fact is that whiteness is not simply skin color in America (or Europe), but a set of mythologies inherited by white writers with which they naturally interpret the universe. Thus a William Styron, a white liberal and winner of a Pulitzer prize for his *Nat Turner,* could not envision a slave (Nat Turner) revolting from natural feelings, but only when his mind was unsettled by an indulgent white. When Styron was ready to show how an untampered-with Black revolts, he created the mindless and savage rapist and slaughterer named Will. Now I would submit that William Styron is a white writer. Imagine a talented Black (who was not simply putting down a fast hustle) using Styron's mythology! Or imagine Richard Wright interpreting the South by some modified version of Faulknerian mythology. We must keep in mind here that we are talking about stances that deeply affect the interpretation of black experience. In this context, Faulkner will everywhere be seen as a white writer.

Now someone will say, but what about a black writer such as Chesnutt? For some time, whites didn't even know he was black.

My answer is that all the situation meant is that white folks thought he was white—a white writer. Now, of course, to many whites, *white writer* is what is meant by *writer.* Further, all one can extract from the Chesnutt situation is that a choice exists for a Black between being a black writer or a white writer—not between being something called simply *writer* and something called *black* writer. Actually, Chesnutt's situation is far more complex than the hypothetical questioner implies. He wrote at a time (turn of the Century) when to get printed by a major publishing house and to hold onto a white audience were to make very grave concessions to white mythology.

Thus there are mythologies of Whites and Blacks that are identifiable, which are really *white* mythologies, particularly in *The House Behind the Cedars,* but, to a lessened degree, also in *The Colonel's Dream* and *The Marrow of Tradition.* One might say that the mythic view of white gentleman and white lady is presented medium rare; a white author would, at that time, have taken it back to the kitchen for cooking to "well-done." There are also specific ideological statements regarding Anglo-Saxonism, but any close reader of Chessnut will have to note that, in addition, Chessnut has a black rhythm going, and that some of his most memorable personages turn out to be minor black characters.

Now some of the adoption of white mythology is probably unconscious for both Chessnut and other writers. Frantz Fanon calls the condition cultural imposition, W. E. B. DuBois in "Of Our Spirituals Strivings," *The Souls of Black Folks,* speaks of "double-consciousness." The latter can take interesting and subtle twists, since to escape the area of brute oppression is to acquire instruments ("education," etc.) that transform one's psychic structure and enforce a greater openness to powerful and subtle mythologies that deny one's existence. Thus, unless one is very lucky and unusally skilled in his foot-work, one effects the *illusion* of escape only and the loss of one's being, or at best considerable modification. Thus, so knowing a man as Richard Wright rages against the murderous weight of the West upon the backs of Blacks, but still flashes forth the lonely posture of the Western ideal; the expression of the individual life as revolutionary will, which also bears the nagging weight of alienation from many of the rhythms of one's own people.

So in some of the essays I'm concerned about double-consciousness and about what I call the *sensibility* of the black writer. The clean adjustment is hard come by, and the struggle for it is what I mean by the title of this book: *Blackness and the Adventure of Western Culture.* It ties in with the business of being a black writer, and acknowledging it, for there are too many other forces working against one's being to take on such silly psychic burdens as denying from the outset one's identity. One becomes Paul Laurence Dunbar presenting mainly the idyllic portions of a tough folk tradition, in conformity with white mythology; and Countee P. Cullen fretting because, try as he may, his Negroness keeps informing the best of his poems.

And what, praise goodness, happens to the complexity, the variety, and density of the black experience while the knee is so bent?

Well, enough. I wish to acknowledge the patient and strategic encouragement of my wife, and the patience of my children. I have benefitted by discussions with many people, particularly audiences of the College Language Association and others who raised issues.

As indicated in formal acknowledgments, some essays collected here first appeared in the *CLA Journal* and *Black World,* and I'm grateful for permission to reprint.

Finally, for certain intellectual stimulation and productive discussions, I wish to offer my thanks to Professors James C. Bruce of the Department of German, and Charles Long of the Department of the History of Religion, University of Chicago.

March 29, 1971

**Blackness
and
the Adventure
of
Western Culture**

Patterns
of the
Harlem Renaissance:

THE SINGLE UNIFYING CONCEPT WHICH PLACES THE achievement of the Harlem Renaissance in focus is that it moved to gain authority in its portrayal of black life by the attempt to assert, with varying degrees of radicality, a dissociation of sensibility from that enforced by American culture and its institutions. As will be seen, the achievement of the writers was the breaking of ground, which left the soil in a much more receptive condition for future tillers. It did not, however, achieve the radical dissociation of sensibility (a dissociation at the roots) which many of today's black writers are attempting to assert.

By the term *sensibility,* I mean the writer's means of sensing, apprehending; his characteristic emotional, psychic, and intellectual response to existence. We may say, for example, that Paul Laurence Dunbar, writing at the turn of the century, retained in his sensibility too much of the nostalgic glow for the lost plantation days, exploited and conferred by such white writers as Thomas Nelson Page and Joel Chandler Harris, to get at the deeper levels of the complexity, density, and variety of the black life of his time. There were, of course, practical problems which reinforced the exercise of such a sensibility: the expectations of a white audience, who largely provided the cash (although his celebrations of the simple delights of black life were enjoyed by a rather sizeable black audience); and the expectations of publishers of magazines and books.

On the positive side, Dunbar, while narrowing the black folk tradition to largely the *idyllic,* infused his poetry with a flowing

17

Library I M C
Champaign Centennial High School
Champaign, Illinois

music and a humanity not available from the white writers. Since blacks are often portrayed as conferring hatred upon each other, it should also be mentioned that Dunbar is not often surpassed in reflecting the joy that Blacks frequently experience in being with each other.

For the Harlem Renaissance, a Dunbar is thus both a precursor, a fact seldom mentioned, and a sensibility against which to revolt. His poetry influenced the early Langston Hughes, and his single novel to focus upon Blacks, *The Sport of the Gods,* a novel with settings both on the plantation and in New York City, influenced the portrayal of city life during the Renaissance.

There are other important precursors, whose sensibilities and works mark out, sometimes by contrast and sometimes by certain similarities, the paths of revolt and engagement that Harlem Renaissance writers reflect. Charles Waddell Chesnutt had strongly reflected definitions from black folk traditions, one of the important resources of the Renaissance, in such works as *The Conjure Woman* (1899), and certain stories in the collection *The Wife of His Youth and Other Stories* (1899). To a lesser degree of effectiveness, Chesnutt handles sharp insights from folk tradition in his novels—the most memorable gestures and characters have it as their source, despite the rituals warmly endorsing the whiteness of several mulatto characters. I would simply point out here that he worked in a tight framework that allowed his racial identity to go, for awhile, unnoticed. Within this framework, he was able to do several things: produce "Baxter's Procrustes," a short story that shows complete mastery of the form, make more use of the folk's supernaturalist and conjure tradition in *The Conjure Woman,* than has since been made of it, and make an effective use of the "fooling massa" folk tradition in such an hilarious short story as "The Passing of Grandeson."

The area which Chesnutt presents for revolt is the devices of his framework which for a brief period were myths of whiteness that appeared in his novels, the exalted position that he gave to the white narrator and his wife in *The Conjure Woman,* and his tendency to associate culture mainly with his light skinned characters.

Because of its concentration upon the working out of the principle that character is fate, its low key presentation of racial propaganda, and its varied portraits of black life, James Weldon John-

18

son's *The Autobiography of an Ex-Coloured Man,* is usually greatly emphasized as a precursor of the Renaissance. It also gives a more penetrating rendering of the psychology of the mulatto character who decides to pass than Chesnutt usually afforded. On the negative side, what students quickly notice is that the hero, who is not forced into a knowledge of racial identity until late in childhood, never becomes black in any psychological or inescapable sense, and the title *Ex-Coloured Man* is, therefore, misleading.

Seldom mentioned as a precursor to the Renaissance is W. E. B. DuBois's *The Souls of Black Folk* (1903), although the book had more impact upon aspiring young Blacks than any other single work. Langston Hughes mentions its inspiration—as does Claude McKay. Several of its essays represent a concern with folk, folk music, and the grim struggle of soul which usually turned out to be its own and only reward. DuBois was later to define the limits of its sensibility—one which asserted confidence in moral suasion, reason, the individual triumph in mastering culture, the possibility of insuring a nobler American racial life through the joint efforts of a black and white aristocracy, etc. His grim, intractable facts often contradict the viability of his sensibility in *Souls of Black Folk,* and he was later to feel that the book would have profited by absorption of Marx's description of the impact of economic motive upon the lives of men and Freud's understanding of the unconscious and the operation of sex within the psyche.

It will be seen so far that powerful personalities and areas of distinctive achievement were preparing the way for a Renaissance in which Blacks would attempt to move with a more secure possession of self. It is necessary now to record some non-literary events whose ferment helped to produce a black consciousness of sufficient magnitude to support the turn in the road which Harlem Renaissance writers were engaged in making.

By 1910, the NAACP had been established, with DuBois as director of publicity and editor of *The Crisis,* a magazine which was to provide a conservative, but fighting, nationalism, and a mass-circulating forum for black writers of the 1920's. In the following year, the National Urban League came into being, and in 1923, its organ *Opportunity* was to provide an outlet for black writers. Besides representing organizational growth, these groups thus afforded what earlier black writers could *not* depend upon: outlets sympathetic to their bent and aims.

From 1916 to 1919, the great migration of Southern Blacks to Northern urban areas was in progress. By 1918, 1,000,000 Blacks were estimated to have left the South, although the North and West in public census showed a net gain of only 333,000. World War I, of course, and the country's closing of the doors to immigrants, made for a labor demand which northern industry attempted to fill by persuading and encouraging black Southerners to immigrate, an act made easier of fulfillment because of injustice in Southern courts, lynchings, discrimination, a severe labor depression in 1914 and 1915, which brought wages down to seventy-five cents per day and less, and 1915 floods which left thousands homeless.

The Pennsylvania Railroad, alone brought 12,000 to work on its tracks—all but 2,000 from Georgia and Florida. Nearly 27,000 Blacks found jobs in shipbuilding, 75,000 in coal mines, 300,000 on railroads. Other industries represent large figures. One additional dramatic change is represented in the fact that 21,457 black women were employed in 75 different tasks in typical industrial plants.

Then World War I provided a large number of black men with an experience abroad in which they seemed, for the first time, to be respected simply as men when white Americans weren't busy corrupting the minds of the French.

The period had its built-in devices for disillusionment. Few black workers were accepted in labor unions. The end of World War I saw extraordinary violence inflicted upon blacks, as whites became uneasy as to how Blacks were going to adjust to post-World War "normalcy." Thus, in what is known as the red summer of 1919, race riots occurred in 25 cities—North, South, East and West. Some of the cities: Washington, D.C., Chicago, Knoxville, Tennessee; Omaha, Nebraska; Tulsa, Oklahoma; and Elaine, Arkansas. During the first year of the post-World War I, whites lynched seventy blacks—ten of the group being soldiers still in uniform. Fourteen Blacks were publicly burned—eleven while still alive.

There were, of course, other discouraging matters that were helping to reform the consciousness of a people into one against which a black writer could test his own. This formation was, itself, a positive thing. As Alain Locke, chief mentor of the Renaissance, has pointed out, Blacks had, heretofore, common problems without a common consciousness.

This consciousness was to acquire further substance through the coming forth of a West Indian nationalist, Marcus Garvey, who was to build a huge mass movement which gave to the ordinary black man greater psychological security in his sense of selfhood and a strong feeling of identity. Asserting that racial prejudice was indemic to a white man's civilization and appeals for justice, therefore, futile; advocating the establishment of a black state, pride in all things Black, self help, racial purity, separatism, and confidence in a glorious African past, Marcus Garvey claimed a black following that numbered in the millions. He also collected millions of dollars, built institutions for his programs, and posed a threat internationally, before he was cut down and deported by the United States government under dubious procedures. His impact on Blacks and the Renaissance was strong, even where poets merely wrote literary versions of an African homeland.

A new assertiveness was abroad. In the riots, more than ever before, the shedding of black blood cost the shedding of white blood. The NAACP had begun to accumulate a string of landmark victories in the courts and to emerge as powerful propagandist and national lobbyist. Out of the greater freedom space provided by the North and the foregoing experiences came the tensions mingling in consciousness, which provided both disillusionment and a greater hope —and the birth of the Black Renaissance.

From white writers came important contributions that widened the area of public acceptance of portrayals of black life. The American public had seen black life as worthy of literary consideration mainly in terms of buffoonery, pathos, or malicious stupidity. The lens was that of minstrel tradition.

Here three white playwrights made a powerful impact. Ridgely Torrence, who felt that black life might produce some of the powerful drama in the world, gave serious treatment to it in three plays that were produced with such black actors as Opal Cooper, Blanche Deas, and Inez Clough. The landmark plays were "Granny Maumee," 'Simon the Cyrenian," and "The Rider of Dreams."

In 1919, from Eugene O'Neill came "The Dreamy Kid," a gangster play and "The Emperor Jones," in which both Charles Gilpin and Paul Robeson, at different times, played the title role. O'Neill followed these two plays with a tragedy of interracial marriage, "All God's Chillun Got Wings."

Paul Green contributed important folk plays, the most outstanding of which was "In Abraham's Bosom," involving the tragic aspirations of a Southern mulatto and featuring such black actors as Julius Bledsoe, Rose McClendon, and Abbie Mitchell. Although the plays hardly gave satisfactory treatment to black lives, they did approach them with a new seriousness and sometimes through a tragic vision.

The playwrights helped to increase the acceptance of serious black actors, but, of course, had little effect in opening the stage to black playwrights, a problem which the Harlem Renaissance did not solve.

In the general American context, it should also be mentioned that the post-World War I period represented a resumption of a questioning attitude on the part of white writers, the presence of a desire to escape from a constricting respectability that promoted an interest in the exotic and primitivism, and some *serious* interest in social and labor problems as evinced by the studies of Frank Tannenbaum and others. Sinclair Lewis's *Main Street* appeared in 1920 and *Babbitt* in 1925. Then there were Theodore Dreiser's *An American Tragedy* in 1925, and other works representative of the roaring twenties and the quest of whites for the primitive, a quest which helped to unlock doors of prestigious publishing houses to black writers who had formerly found the doors locked, barred, and bolted.

The foregoing formed the setting and commingling tensions that buzzed in what is known as the Harlem Renaissance. We may now have a general look at some personalities before focussing upon specific authors and issues. As we move into the discussion, it will be good to keep in mind that we are entering a period where all the arts, not merely the literary, boomed, although this essay is confined to a consideration of literary issues.

II

The array of personalities in the literary area is startling. Few were born in New York, although we speak of a Harlem Renaissance. Claude McKay, one of the movement's ornaments, was born in Jamaica, Eric Walrond, short story writer, in British Guiana.

Others such as Langston Hughes and Arna Bontemps represent Kansas and Louisiana and California.

Most bore credentials of a talented tenth, though some were able to allow the credentials to hang very loose. The older shepherds, mentors, and sometime contributors brought both formal credentials and a cosmopolitanism that few Americans could match. W. E. B. DuBois, scholar and editor of *The Crisis,* reflected an old time yankee New England upbringing, a Fisk-Harvard American education, with a Ph.D. as his terminal degree and study in European universities. By the time of the Renaissance, he was already a scholar and intellectual leader of world stature.

Alain Locke, who was to provide brilliant criticism and interpretation: Harvard Ph.D. and Rhodes Scholar, a most cosmopolitan man.

Charles S. Johnson, editor of *Opportunity,* educational background—The University of Chicago, eventually a distinguished scholar in the social sciences and President of Fisk University.

James Weldon Johnson—product of a cultivated family and Atlanta University, a musical composer, novelist, poet, educator, diplomat: Again a most cosmopolitan man.

In the younger group, there was also the evidence of considerable formal education, and cosmopolitaen experience through travel and varied cultural contacts. Claude McKay derived from a very British oriented school system and further study at Tuskegee and Kansas State University. It should be added of course that McKay had an across-the-board contact with both the masses and advanced political and literary circles, as reflected in his autobiography, *A Long Way from Home.*

Langston Hughes, who perhaps had the greatest range of contact with the masses and all manner of men, was eventually a graduate of Lincoln University. Both Hughes and McKay had lived the lives they sang of in their songs. But McKay's *apartness* is always clearly evident and his role as the cultivated bohemian and radical is carried with a flourish. Hughes seems easily to exemplify a natural identification with the masses, to be a sort of born "everyman." But it is also to be noted that a reading of his autobiographies *The Big Sea* and *I Wonder As I Wander* does not exactly unlock the privacy of his soul.

Rudolph Fisher, B.A. and M.A. Brown University, M.D. Howard University, specialist in Roentgenology, exemplified in his novels and short stories a very intimate and sophisticaed contact with the range of blacks and whites of the period.

Perhaps a greater rigidity of class background is exemplified by Jean Toomer, a product of the University of Wisconsin, with further study at City College, N.Y., and Kansas State University; and by Jessie Fanset, the novelist and poet devoted to the more secure groups of blacks, who was a graduate of Cornell, with further study in France. However, Toomer's *Cane* reveals both the exiled narrator and a considerable grasp of a broad range of black characters. Certainly, in *Cane*, his own difference from his characters seems to provide just the right tension for insight, although it may also be a source of excessive poeticizing.

Now one can continue to run down college degrees and special cultivation with a large number of the stars of the Renaissance: Fenton Johnson, Arna Bontemps, Frank Horne, and especially Countee P. Cullen. Cullen because the symbols of middle class respectability do seem awesome and controlling—from the elaborate religious background through such matters as the New York University-Harvard education and his social register marriage to W. E. B. DuBois's daughter. The marriage as described by Blanche Ferguson in *Countee Cullen and the Negro Renaissance* seems a special kind of flight from reality.

But my point is not a simple put down of Renaissance figures as "bourgies" lacking relevance to the people whose struggles and qualities they were to portray. I am simply trying to get into one basket the sense of a variety of tensions modifiable by highly individual personalities.

On the positive side, their status gave them a certain psychological poise—a perspective from which they could not easily be overawed by definitions of black realities provided by American and Western culture. As Blacks active during the 1920's, their education would not automatically separate them from other Blacks. Indeed, the 1920's provided still a solid racial boxing in that required that if a Black was to get away from other Blacks, he would have to work at it, make a special job of it. Despite W. E. B. DuBois's famous reticence, a study of his range of contact with backwoods Blacks at certain periods of his life would probably reveal some very startling statistics.

The heavyweight middle class symbols do have their negative side. It comes quickly into focus, if a couple of the more absolute principles which Ralph Ellison was espousing in the 1940's are applied: that the black writer, if he is to be effective must move his own consciousness beyond the furtherest reach of bourgeois consciousness; and that techniques must be both a reflection and an instrument of consciousness. Ellison seems to mean that one must achieve a freedom from the mythologies which inform the vision of the white middle class if one is to see fully the contours of the black image, and that technique must be equal to the complexity of one's awareness.

Now I have already suggested that many Harlem Renaissance writers brought to their task a cosmopolitanism and a wide range of experience which protected them from a simple myopia of a middle class perspective. By looking at individuals, we can see the degree to which some artistic freedom resulted, and we should add to the writer's trump card their recourse to bohemianism.

Claude McKay, for example, struck the first powerful Renaissance notes. In 1919, he published the famous sonnet, "If We Must Die" in *The Liberator,* the magazine of bohemian radicalism. The sonnet, a call to Blacks to meet violence with violence, evidenced a new ease with poetic form, a newly achieved psychological freedom, and McKay's ability to bend traditional forms to his purpose. Further, he was aware of the sonnet's social and other traditions. Evident in poems of *Harlem Shadows* (1922) and subsequent poetry was a sensibility freer than that of most Harlem Renaissance writers, one that could flash forth an absolute sense of manhood and celebrate or defy with tenderness or a blazing anger. In major fictional works, such as *Home to Harlem* (1928), *Banjo* (1929), and *Banana Bottom* (1933), he showed a grasp of the big picture of black life and an extensive range of contact.

Still, as with other brilliant writers of the Renaissance, one feels a *potential* greatness that is not quite achieved. His poetry, including "If We Must Die," which according to his autobiography *A Long Way from Home,* moved his fellow dining car workers to tears, remains splendid beauties in a medium sized room. Though he deals with ordinary black life, the center of his poems is really their speaker of cultivated sensibility—a natural aristocrat. The fiction celebrates the vitality and beauty of Blacks, but McKay raises questions of national significance only to resolve them by sentimental endings that do not really resolve. The form of soul is frequently bohemianism.

I would suggest that McKay was unable to achieve sufficient freedom from his early British oriented education, that his bohemianism permeated his radicalism, and that a sense of individual apartness left him open to one of the more neutralizing forms of middle class reaches—romantic individualism. Such handicaps were a barricade between him and ultimate realization of his potential, despite his additional armor of socialism and radical politics.

Jean Toomer, whose *Cane* (1923) is a group of narratives and poetry that continues to amaze people, allows us to say little more than the fact that the book, itself, bears the mark of greatness. But following it Toomer abandoned Blacks as a literary subject. From biographical reports and his own autobiographical comment, it is clear that he was very much moved by the *range* of philosophical possibility in the idea of identity. In *Cane,* his Southern rural characters retain a kind of *wholeness* and *richness* of soul, although there is no viable avenue for the soul's fulfillment. His more northward situated characters suffer from attenuation of soul under the impact of modern industrialism and respectability. His subject is the thwarted fulfillment of the soul.

Toomer may have represented the kind of racial consciousness that for a brief interval is *most* intense *precisely* because it is about to *disappear.* We should perhaps be thankful that he rendered this intensity with such great artistic power before he gave up his racial identity—or merged it, as he would have seen the situation.

Cane is a storehouse of contemporary techniques. Perhaps one vestige of Toomer's middle classness, however, is the distance of the narrator from several of the characters. But it can hardly be said to *block* him from a sense of their *beauty.*

Langston Hughes, whose poetry in *The Weary Blues* (1926) and *Fine Clothes to the Jew* (1927), displays a talent that had great impact, reflects in his autobiographies *The Big Sea* and *I Wonder As I Wander* a well worked out grasp of his task and times. In 1926 in the famous manifesto, "The Negro Artist and the Racial Mountain," he attacked the tendency of middle class Blacks to suppress their black selves and heritage in an uncritical embrace of whiteness, and announced his commitment to the lowdown blacks where the richness of the black soul remained uncorrupted.

His images of the low-down Blacks in his manifsto are over-saturated with romantic bohemianism, and do not really get at the workaday world in which most Blacks are embattled. But they do show a move away from middle class consciousness. It was a good first step, and Hughes was to continue to grow. Arthur P. Davis, in his essay "The Harlem of Langston Hughes' Poetry," included in Gross and Hardy's *Images of the Negro in American Literature,* has traced a shift of focus from uncritical celebrations of black vitality and joy to confrontations with the grimmer aspects of black life, from which a deep spiritual beauty emerges.

Hughes backed up his revolt by considerable experimentation with forms derived from black folk culture and adapted in the modern city. The forms, themselves, contain stances toward existence, and their value for the self-conscious writer is *not* in their quaintness but in their *forms of response to existence* and their spiritual beauty and other implications. Thus he invested his poetry with the inner spirit of the blues, spirituals, folk ballads, and gospel songs. From a deceptive simplicity arises powerful suggestions concerning the variety and complexity of the black experience. He, of course, did extraordinary work in other forms.

But what I'm trying to suggest is that he was sufficiently involved through the folk forms in an *alternative* to white or black middle class consciousness to gain an elaborate sense of black life.

Hughes is one of the lasting fruits of the Renaissance, and we forget that a movement is finally measured by a few men who persist and realize its potentialities. Hughes's complexity is even more difficult to suggest in a few lines than that of Claude McKay. He gave folk and cultural tradition a greater rendering power than it had had before in self-conscious literature. His use of blues form and jazz rhythms was the major innovation in black poetry of the Harlem Renaissance, and his alliance with free verse provided him with the benefit of a form known for flexibility and freedom from rigid implications and limitations of the more restricted verse. Hughes has cumulative impact, and, if read with a sure sense of the implications of folk culture in mind, reveals discoveries not yet domesticated by the public. To illustrate: his novel *Not Without Laughter,* though flawed, attempts to embody, separately and then combined, the blues and spirituals traditions; and his short play "Soul Gone Home" reaches into religious and supernaturalist sources.

Hughes's main limitation is that, for whatever reason, he remained too close to the folk forms and did not take the liberty to force upon them as much signification as they could be made to bear.

Countee Cullen's lyric gift is well recognized, and the prevailing dictum is that his poems involved with race are probably his best, although he did not want to be judged as a Negro poet. Although one seldom feels that Cullen has arrived at a point of unfamiliar ground in the official black middle class perspective by which he was surrounded, his gift was that he could say things in a music that was *beyond* pre-1920's achievement. He suffers, of course, by placing himself within the shadow of Keats. But one has conveyed from his first volume of poetry *Color* (1925) a skill with traditional forms that he did not lose, even if he did not seem to attain much of the continued growth that was expected. On the negative side, Cullen's cultivated speaker in his poems seems to provide too little variation in modulations for the situations he described.

"Heritage," his most famous poem, for example, asks What is Africa to me, and gives a rundown of standard *public* images of Africa and finally a criticism of the necessity to worship a white god, but the speaker's highly cultivated tones, as beautiful as they are, do *not* convey a sense of the grittiness of the situation. One must locate the poem's conflict in a cultivated speaker's feeling of alienation, and not with any specifics concerning a *real* Africa. As Stephen Bronz points out in *The Roots of Negro Racial Consciousness*, Cullen's preoccupation with beauty is rendered largely through sound and color.

For the rest of the Renaissance, Cullen was to continue publishing poems that represent fine expression, without going beyond his earlier work and without meeting sterner tests provided by his master John Keats: concreteness and economy deeply communicating the tension of a tragic vision.

In the novel *One Way to Heaven* (1932), Cullen provides delightful satire on religion and black upper class pretensions, although it is apparent today that he knew some of his key characters *only* well enough to provide a middle level of seriousness. He had the possibilities of a great novel developing through the characters

28

of Sam, his wife Mattie, and his wife's mother. They are powerful figures of black tradition: Sam, as the religious trickster and rounder; his wife as an uneasy container of black religious tensions, the mother as one who is able to combine them with a direct confrontation with the vitality of life.

However, Cullen needed to be able to analyze both Sam and his wife at great˙ depths, instead he gives us types, a procedure that works well with his upper class black characters toward whom his attitude is consistently satirical. But he invites the reader to a journey of discovery, in the case of the lower class characters, and then cuts short the journey.

Bronz and others have seen Cullen as violating his principles of showing only the more pleasant and respectable sides of black life. But the unsavory aspects are so well distanced and the respectable, though satirized, so much at the foreground, that such a judgment does *not seem* serious.

Cullen thus represents the triumph of the middle class consciousness. And his fineness must be enjoyed within it. He brings us to other writers usually immediately placed within the ultra-respectable group: Jessie Fanset, Nella Larsen, and Georgia Douglass Johnson, along with such older persisting writers as DuBois and James Weldon Johnson, and Walter White.

Ironically, they, as Cullen does not, suggest that very significant distinctions and certain revisions of judgments may occur as we *restudy* them. Fanset, Larsen, and Walter White, the famous head of the NAACP, are frequently placed in a category labeled "Themes of upper class respectability and passing across the color line," with "propaganda" further defining Walter White's *The Fire in the Flint*. However, Fanset deserves restudy for her concern with character and reflection of a class. A re-reading of Nella Larsen today suggests that, despite the fact that her novels *Quicksand* and *Passing*, deal with some light skinned characters who pass for white, the author's real interest was to test the characters of Blacks whose cultural circumstances provided a high level of choices. Larsen, also, in *Quicksand*, used, effectively and unsentimentally, sharp contrasting pictures from folk tradition.

I am not sure that under re-study her stature would increase beyond that given to her by Robert Bone in *The Negro Novel in America*, but some valuable light on the Renaissance may be shed by a more accurate critical description of her intentions. Certainly one regrets that she did not write more novels and senses that she had a complexity of awareness that might have produced great works. Her work suggests that she had taken more than passing notice of Henry James and Edith Wharton.

As to Walter White, one might recur to the description of his handling the passing-for-white theme given in Sterling Brown and others, *The Negro Caravan*, which suggests White's intimate rendering of the subject and the variety of his portraiture. Georgia Douglass Johnson, who wrote mainly conventional but competent lyrics about a woman's life, could be more concretely engaged and described. W. E. B. DuBois, who in *The Quest of the Silver Fleece* (1910), wrote with a rather challenging depth of social reference, labors, as a creative writer, under the shadow of himself as scholar and propagandist. His criticism in *The Crisis* of the 1920's does give evidence of viewing literature as uplift instrument, but other critical comments by him would hardly seem so easily categorized. DuBois does not hesitate to be propagandistic as evidenced by his Renaissance novel *Dark Princess*. But a study which carefully sorted out his varied tensions and took into consideration imaginative works that do not fall within simple genre categories would give us a more confident estimate of his literary stature. He was *hardly* a man to be contained by simple categories.

James Weldon Johnson's brilliant creative achievement for the Renaissance resides in the volume of seven folk sermons rendered in poetry without heavy reliance upon dialect, and in the reissuance of his pre-Renaissance novel, *The Autobiography of an Ex-Colored Man*, which gained more attention during the Renaissance than it had attracted before. Johnson's cosmopolitanism always extended his reach and his grasp. The sermons are beautiful still. We would do well, however, to study the sermons in comparison with actual folk sermons, in order to give stronger authority to our critical judgment, since the obligation of the self-conscious writer is to carry us to a different sort of awareness than that provided by the folk. The folk form, that is, should increase the distinction of the new thing that the self-conscious writer makes out of it. An outstanding example of its potentiality is Ellison's use of the True Blood Narrative in *Invisible Man*.

We will have to return briefly to James Weldon Johnson *as critic*, after looking at a few individuals who are not easily attachable to preceding groups. Eric Walrond in *Tropic Death* (1926), a series of short stories on Caribbean life, reveals an ability to get inside black life and render it through sharply etched images and a dialect that carries voice tones.

Rudolph Fisher, who had the lightest touch of all the Renaissance writers, managed an intermingling of kindly satire and bittersweet tensions in his fiction. Although he is well known for his novels, *The Walls of Jericho* (1928), which presents a cross section of black life, and *The Conjure Man Dies* (1932), in which he begins a black tradition of the detective story, it is in such short stories as "Miss Cynthia," "The City of Refuge," and "High Yaller," that he achieves a tight form that renders some of the plight of the newly arrived Southern migrant and the tensions of color caste. In such a novel as *The Walls of Jericho,* we have good fun and pictures of life that grow serious, but are held in check by a middle class sense of hearty good will, exemplified by an author expert at pulling strings.

The short stories approach the stark threat of life in the destruction of the idealistic Southern migrant in "The City of Refuge" and the hard choices forced by the tensions of color caste in "High Yallar." Once again one feels oneself in the presence of a writer of potential greatness. Unfortunately, Fisher died at the age of 37, so it cannot fairly be said where his talents would have led him. During his brief life, he gave us pictures of the ordinary workaday Black who was *largely neglected* by other Renaissance writers.

Wallace Thurman, who is perhaps most famous for his bitter satire of the Renaissance in the novel *Infants of the Spring* (1932), deserves some *re-examination* for the potentiality of his novel *The Blacker the Berry,* whose heroine Emma Lou fights the battle of intraracial color prejudice. Although his novel halts, rather than ends, it deserves greater credit for character analysis than it has been given. His play "Harlem" and his short story "Cordelia the Crude," which appeared in the briefly lived magazine *Fire,* also give some grim pictures of Harlem which other writers usually ignored. In the November, 1970, issue of *Black World,* Dorothy West in her memoir "Elephant's Dance" portrays him as a gifted person whose unresolved personal tensions fed a fatal bohemianism. Thurman died of tuberculosis and dissipation at the age of 32.

The above writers, with perhaps the addition of George S. Schuyler, the Menckenite satirist in his novel *Black No More,* will represent main patterns of the Renaissance. A *fuller* picture is gained by recognition of authors who established their rights to ground during the Renaissance, but reached the highest point of their careers afterward. This achievement usually meant that they were adaptable to tensions of succeeding periods, such as the Great Depression and its aftermath.

Thus Arna Bontemps whose published work during the Renaissance included a substantial group of poems in Countee Cullen's *Caroling Dusk* and elsewhere went on to produce more poetry, outstanding novels, including pioneer work in the historical novel, and to become the distinguished man of letters that we are aware of today.

Zora Neale Hurston published short stories that reflected a close engagement with folk tradition, but her distinguished novels and brilliant book-length folklore studies were to come later. She still awaits the thorough-going critical analysis that will properly place her in the patterns of American fiction.

Sterling Brown was to demonstrate his sophisticated grasp of folk tradition, as well as other traditions, in *Southern Road* (1930), and was to make his mark as a distinguished critic. Like Zora Neale Hurston, he is *yet* to receive the critical attention that he deserves. It is also shocking that *Southern Road,* which goes beyond Renaissance preoccupations to concern itself with tensions of the 1930's and deeper notes of black life, has not yet been reprinted.

The Harlem Renaissance was particularly fortunate in two powerful critics, who also have not yet been systematically assessed: James Weldon Johnson and Alain Locke. Both possessed something much beyond a parochial enthusiasm and cosmopolitan sensitivity, and were able to make incisive judgments.

Johnson's contributions are particularly noteworthy in the prefaces to his two volume collection of spirituals, *The Book of American Negro Spirituals* (1925), and *The Second Book of Negro Spirituals* (1926). His brilliant anthology, *The Book of American Negro Poetry* (1921, revised, 1931) also contains in its preface and headnotes extremely important criticism, concerning the limitations of the dialect poetry of his time and his *Black Manhattan* (1930) is a very important source-book for the study of black drama.

Alain Locke, best known for the brilliant anthology, *The New Negro* (1925), despite his essentially middle class sensibility and somewhat simplistic integrationist orientation, reflected a critical and cultural sensitivity that has not been surpassed. It is difficult to imagine the Renaissance without his services, critical and otherwise. Perhaps it should be said that he, in a stream of books and articles, expressed the most *rounded* view of black culture.

Both men tended to express an excessive optimism, but neither lacked the sharp incisive phrase.

What finally does the Harlem Renaissance add up to in terms of achievement?

We must, in order to weigh its outcomes properly, acknowledge two facts: that today it bears the burden of heavy critical strictures, and that these strictures are, to some degree, an acknowledgment of its role as the father of many children, whose features are likely to be looked upon suspiciously by the offspring.

But its negative criticism arose during its own time, and included participants in the movement. Alain Locke, its chief mentor, was eventually to see it as insufficiently socially conscious. Claude McKay was to repudiate his earlier fiction as he turned to Catholicism, and to describe the Renaissance as concerned more with racial uplift, superficial white acceptance, superficial values, than representing its own people or becoming something for them.

Langston Hughes, in *The Big Sea,* was to see the movement as a time when fun was to be had by all, but also as a rebirth whose good news the ordinary Black never heard of—and would not have had much time for anyway.

Then there was the bitter satire of its bohemianism, hustling and confusion, by Wallace Thurman, in *Infants of the Spring.*

Allison Davis, today a famous sociologist, and Sterling Brown, saw as serious limitations of the movement its failure to dramatize the deeper qualities recognizable in ordinary black people: fortitude, courage, and endurance.

Ralph Ellison has pointed out that it represented an ironic picture: a literature that was still a bawling infant choosing *decadence* as its model for expression. A judgment that is part of the charge that it swung open all doors to entry by whites questing for the exotic and the primitive. In this ritual, white Carl Van Vechten, through his novel *Nigger Heaven,* frequently is seen as a subverter of the fiction into the paths of blatant sexuality and sensationalism.

Harold Cruse, in *Crisis of the Negro Intellectual,* saw it as lacking a true forum for hammering out a common platform or a salon for promoting intellectual excitement. In place of the cultivated and devoted woman of the arts, such as Mabel Dodge could be for whites in Greenwich Village, the Renaissance had Aleila Walker, a vital black woman who inherited a fortune from the hair straightening enterprises of her mother. In her great parties, good eating, good drinking, and good publishing contacts in an area too tightly packed with people to provide overall group communion seem to have been the main advantages.

And today's young writers, while conceding that the Renaissance left them a foundation, look askance at its failure to build lasting institutions and to truly address itself to a black audience.

Certainly, a good deal of the movement is placed in perspective when we realize that, while the Marcus Garvey nationalist movement and the blues were allowed to make injections, they seemed to remain for most Renaissance writers superficial diversions, bastard brothers and sisters, lovable even in certain ways, but not eligible for Sunday company or a real dining room kind of intimacy.

It must be admitted that all charges are supportable, in varying degrees, but that some seem more applicable to a part of the Renaissance than to the whole. As a single example, Ellison's charge of decadence, is more applicable to certain novels and stories than to poetry. What is needed is a very exhaustive study of all forces operating within the period, so that properly weighted judgment and completely accurate descriptions can be provided.

Meanwhile, we must acknowledge several accomplishments that were *fundamental.*

Certainly, no genre of literature went without substantial development. The short story in the hands of Toomer, Eric Walrond, and Langston Hughes, became a much more flexible form for that moment of illumination of black life. The novel, while not freed from the episodic structure or audible spasms in plot movement, provided memorable analyses that occasionally stopped just short of greatness. And the drama, while sneaking only occasionally through barricades to Broadway prominence as in the cases of Hall

34

Johnson's *Run Little Children,* and Wallace Thurman's *Harlem,* made progress in little theater and folk drama not known before, and the minstrel tradition was mortally wounded.

Although the loss of white patronage resulting from the stock market crash critically wounded the movement, it produced writers who were to persist and whose consciousnesses were to become an essential metaphor for black realities of subsequent periods as they remained open to new tensions.

What we can see today, after all charges have been recorded, is that the Renaissance made paths through what had been stubborn thickets. It put muscles on non-literary institutions, such as newspapers, the Urban League, the NAACP, labor leadership, which, however we may now categorize them ideologically, were to become powerful weight lifters. From a literary point of view, it made a strategic turn at the forks of the road.

As I said at the beginning, its dissociation of sensibility from constraining definitions enforced by white middle class culture, though not radical, was essential, was a stronger grasp of the black selfhood which W. E. B. DuBois had described as under threat from the Blacks' double consciousness: the consciousness enforcing white definitions upon him; and the part that desired a full embrace of the universe.

If today, we can sometimes jog, rather than puff, down the road toward self definition, it would seem that the Harlem Renaissance was a father who should not go without thanks or reverence.

The
Soulful Way
of Claude McKay

FOR McKAY, HIMSELF, SOUL WAS THE ASSERTION OF A
naturalness of being to be maintained in the face of the most complex patterns of Western culture. Absorbing what was inescapable
in Western culture and what must be mastered in order to live in
the "modern" world, he attempted to develop from within. That is,
he wished to draw into himself strands of Western culture that
agreed with his own rhythms, but not to be shook by its devitaliz-
ing vibrations—its tendency to be the blow-fly corrupting impulses
derived from healthy and close association of man with his fellows
and with the deepest rhythms of land, water, and sky. Both his autobiography *A Long Way from Home* and his novel *Banana Bottom*
reveal that the struggle is made upon a rocky road.

As to the masses of Blacks, McKay felt in them a warmth, an
assertion of spirit in the face of pain, a bounce and spontaneity of
feelings and emotions, and a striving for the fruits of life based
upon deep and persistent responses to the rhythms of their universe.
He tried to insist, despite threatening evidence to the contrary, that
the ordinary Black possessed an instinctive healthiness and innocence
which would secure him from the waves of corruption that pound-
ed into his cage in Western culture.

What McKay brought to the Harlem Renaissance then was the
attempt to project a positive *niggerhood*—a voice that could celebrate or defy with apparent simple directness. McKay's voice was
heard first in his poetry in America just a few years prior to the

Renaissance, although his first book publications abroad occurred in 1912, *Songs of Jamaica* and *Constab's Ballads*. In the early works his distinctive achievement had been dialect poems, which expressed a rugged but tender soulfullness in black Jamaican life.

In 1919, his voice smashed through a sound barrier in America, with the appearance of the explosive and famous sonnet "If We Must Die." From a black poet America had not heard its like before, although McKay had published poems here under a pseudonym in 1917. An answering snarl to the 1919 race riots, the poem aroused Senator Henry Cabot Lodge to read it into the Congressional Record as evidence of Negro radicalism. It gained a black audience, whose deep emotions and post-World War I spirit of defiance were at the heart of its explosive lines, and it was reprinted in black newspapers and magazines. Paradoxically, the poem bore a form validated by centuries of European culture, the Shakesperian sonnet. *Harlem Shadows,* 1922, the book of poems that clearly pointed to the incipient Renaissance, also exploited traditional forms, and reflected an author who could render the illusion of being completely present in his emotions, whether raging or tender. Thus the most radical sounding voice of the Renaissance is projected from the most traditional forms.

Any number of simple explanations can be given for McKay's poetic situation, but I prefer to focus here upon those which most illuminate McKay, the man and poet. This approach requires a closer examination of his sensibility, and his thrust in poetry and in prose.[1]

By *sensibility,* I mean the writer's means of sensing; his *characteristic* emotional, psychic, and intellectual response to existence.

McKay's Jamaican background provided him with a source of sensibility that gave him certain advantages over American born black writers. On the other hand, the circumstances of American born black writers provided a peculiarly intimate knowledge of oppression amidst the massive presence of whites and a variety of survival devices developed through historical tradition.

First, the positive advantages of McKay.

He grew up among a black peasantry in Jamaica, West Indies. Here village life was controlled largely by the peasants—not directly by the symbols associated in America with white plantation owners, the power structure of Western small or big towns, or the impersonal forces of Northern industrialism. McKay makes the distinctions in his autobiography *A Long Way from Home,* and no doubt romanticizes them to a degree. However, they can, I think, be given the necessary qualifications by comparing them with the Jamaica that he describes at different points in his book, *Harlem: Negro Metropolis.*

McKay's father was a figure of authority in the village, where the rhythms of life were expressed in deep friendships among the youth and in imperatives drawn from a closely knit people. When McKay's father became disenchanted with the white head of the local religious mission, he quit the church. Then he and other Blacks compelled the missioner's dismissal.

McKay thus emphasizes in his autobiography that his early background did not permit the development of the imposing myth implied in America by such deeply rooted expressions as "mah whitefolks" or the more sophisticated adaptation, my white friend. White man, I deduce, was not *The Man*—that terribly mythic expression which seems to work its juju upon both humble and "radical" Blacks.

Now in *Harlem: Negro Metropolis,* McKay felt that West Indians in America tended to exaggerate both their background of freedom and their British patriotism. It seems reasonable to assume, nonetheless, that his early background in Jamaica tended not to compel a confrontation with the stark and brutal evidence of black powerlessness which produces the knotted *niggerhood* which so many black Americans struggle solitarily to unravel.

McKay's mind was first "discovered" and cultivated by his own brother, a school teacher and lay minister. By the time that Jekyll, the philanthropic white Englishman, appeared to assist, McKay, through his brother, had already encountered free-thinking writers, a variety of poets and novelists, and had written dialect poetry.

James Weldon Johnson, who was at war with the oppressive and dehumanizing tradition that encrusted the American development of dialect poetry, pointed out the peculiar freedom that McKay was able to exercise in the use of this medium in *Songs of Jamaica,* 1912.

> . . . they are free from both the minstrel and plantation traditions, free from exaggerated sweetness and wholesomeness; they

are veritable impressions of Negro life in Jamaica. Indeed, some of these dialect poems are decidedly militant in tone. It is of course clear to see that McKay had the advantage of not having to deal with stereotypes. He found his medium fresh and plastic.[2]

Johnson has in mind that the American black poet Paul Laurence Dunbar, writing in the late 19th and early 20th Centuries, had to attempt to render black images through a dialect medium which, through its use by white poets, had developed rigid associations with nostalgia for an idealized plantation darky or the antics of white minstrel tradition.

This American dialect medium, Johnson felt, tended to be capable of only two "stops": pathos or humor.[3] The "stops" could neither represent the spread of definitions of reality afforded by black folk and cultural tradition nor the density, variety, and complexity of American black life. I would suggest that Claude McKay's achievement with dialect in 1912 reflected an artistic freedom in Jamaica that could not become meaningfully available to most American black poets until such writers as Langston Hughes and Sterling Brown could make a sufficient dissociation from the sensibility enforced by white American culture.

McKay's development of sensibility under less embattled conditions than those confronting American born black writers made certain rejections and perceptions easier. The furore over whether a black man was to be a black poet or just "a poet" which seemed to consume much psychic energy from many American black writers gave him no trouble. It seemed to him that to refuse to be a black writer if one was black was to reject one's identity. It was a false issue, simply silly, since non-black writers used their own racial identity as an asset.

Although he paid tribute to the value of religion in several fine poems ("A Prayer," "Truth," "The Pagan Isms," "St. Isaac's Church, Petrograd," etc.), he easily formulated the dehumanizing thrust of the West and the irreducible corruption of Western Christianity: ". . . I said [to Frank Harris, English writer and editor] that I thought that the adoption of the Christ cult by Western civilization was its curse: it gave modern civilization its hypocritical facade, for its existence depended upon force and positive exploitation, whereas Jesus was weak and negative."[4]

McKay saw that Blacks must distinguish between segregation and aggregation, and use aggregation for the development of what is now called black power. Prophetically, he stated that Blacks must, themselves, develop a group soul. His conviction is behind his criticism of phoniness and delusion that he saw in the attitudes of some Harlem Renaissance writers: naive assumptions that white financial generosity would be indefinitely available; that acceptance of black art by whites was evidence of steps taken toward social integration; that black art was a racial uplift instrument through its public relations value; and that for the artist merely to be Harlem conscious implied a sufficient appreciation and grasp of black values.

He complained that each black writer "wanted to be the first Negro, the one Negro, and the only Negro *for the whites,* instead of for their own group."[5] Such attitudes also received the frown and smirk of satire in Wallace Thurman's *Infants of the Spring,*[6] a fact that shows that McKay's attack is here too inclusive. Also, a Langston Hughes seemed knowing enough, in the light of Hughes's analysis of the Harlem Renaissance.[7]

For much of his life McKay's sensibility was a black consciousness that seemed to come naturally, even down to emphasizing black control and development of black communities and, in *Harlem: Negro Metropolis,* 1940, to attacking divisive integrationist tactics. Near the end of his life, poverty-stricken and health broken, he turned to Catholicism and repudiated his fiction, but by that time the work for which he is known had been completed, and our concern at this point is with the sensibility which shaped his works.[8]

I have dwelled so far upon the strength that McKay's early background and development gave to his sensibility. Yet one senses that the exceptional nature of McKay's position also led him into romantic individualism—one of the more neutralizing forms of Western personality. Bronz's judgment seems pertinent: "To whatever groups he [McKay] allied himself, McKay remained always something of an outsider without deep and lasting commitment."[9] Thus despite his connections with radicals, closeness to left-wing movements, and his celebrated visit to Russia, where he consorted with masters of the revolution, his discussions of art and politics in his autobiography reveal no sense of their relations. Even his discussions of the artist do not arise above simple copybook maxims concerning the integrity of the artist as an individual, the necessity for high quality writing, and the possibility of a proletarian period in writing.[10]

At the end of his autobiography, McKay states his desire to celebrate a modern Negro leader in verse, and adds: "For I have nothing to give but my singing. All my life I have been a troubadour wanderer, nourishing my self mainly on the poetry of existence. And all I offer here is the distilled poetry of my experience."[11] This romantic stance of the individual nourishing himself on the poetry of existence intrudes upon McKay's very serious moments and attenuates their quality. It seems to make for a kind of romantic egoism that produces solitariness where kinship with larger issues and people is required, and a startling myopia. The result is divisive tensions: rhythms of a natural black style, romantic rebellion, bohemian estheticism, egoism, and a sharp realistic social vision, uneasily commingling.

Thus, although the communists were wide open for McKay's counterattack upon them for their approach to fiction, he chose to defend his portrait of Jake in *Home to Harlem* on the ground of "class consciousness." If one has read *Home to Harlem* he recognizes the virtues of Jake, but the least of them is class consciousness in any ideological sense. McKay's conflict with Michael Gold, eventually a stubborn and doughty communist, regarding editorial policy of *The Liberator* is given in such personal terms that the reader can conclude only that neither, at the time, belonged at the head of the class.

Other than the socialist and communist movements, McKay had available as an instrument of radical social change the Garvey black nationalist development that attracted so many Blacks. But one reads McKay's autobiography and his *Harlem: Negro Metropolis*, without discovering insights that are not all too easily available elsewhere. In *A Long Way from Home*, Garvey is "A West Indian charlatan [who] came to this country, full of antiquated social ideas; yet within a decade he aroused the social consciousness of the Negro masses more than any leader ever did."[12] In *Harlem: Negro Metropolis*, McKay gives a sympathetic account of Garvey and the movement; the word "charlatan" disappears, but McKay is dependent for final judgment upon the conclusions of James Weldon Johnson in *Black Manhattan*.[13]

But one may go on in this attempt to suggest the complex sensibility of McKay. The point is that the virtues and the contradictions intimately affect the stature he was able to achieve.

II

His sonnets are usually credited with representing his highest point of achievement in poetry. In general, they are best when they do not evoke the specific name of one of the masters of romantic tradition, or make obvious a standard romantic posture—standard dangers in working a well-tilled tradition.

This "best" group of sonnets involves a deep souled speaker, who powerfully opposes his inner togetherness to terrible hatred and oppression. Even the speaker in "If We Must Die," the poem that seemed to be an address to the masses of Blacks and whose rage is a response to the violent riots and lynchings of post-World War I, proceeds from this highly developed personality. The speaker calls upon a people to register its nobility of soul by fighting and dying heroically while under attack by foes that far outnumber it —characterized as "monsters" and "the murderous, cowardly pack." The poem came at a time when black people most needed it for their shaken morale. Overnight, it made McKay the poet-hero of black people. Working on the railroad at the time and stopping in strange cities and towns where riot or murder could come suddenly, McKay gave birth to the poem in an explosion of feeling, and thus found that he had struck a common chord.

> . . . for it the Negro people unanimously hailed me as a poet. Indeed that one grand outburst is their sole standard of appraising my poetry. It was the only poem I ever read to the members of my crew [dining car]. They were all agitated. Even the fourth waiter—who was the giddiest and most irresponsible of the lot, with all his motives and gestures colored by a strangely acute form of satyriasis—even he actually cried.[14]

One of the workers urged him to go to Liberty Hall, the headquarters of the Garvey back-to-Africa movement, and read the poem, but McKay was not "uplifted with his enthusiasm for the

Garvey movement," and side-stepped the request by saying "truth-fully that I had no ambition to harrangue a crowd."

This response of the dining-car crew seems to mark a crucial moment in McKay's poetic career. Had he been able to face crowds, he might have been able to draw upon their vast emotional reservoir of Blackness, but having expressed himself and the souls of Blacks simultaneously, he permitted his tendency toward individual apart-ness to take over. He sought Frank Harris, the white English critic who had earlier rejected his sonnet, "The Lynching," and advised McKay that in the sonnet he must "storm heaven" as Milton did in "On the Late Massacre in Piedmont." Frank Harris informed him that he had, indeed, risen to the heights and stormed heaven.

I do not mean to suggest that McKay failed to turn the right corner in his career by not joining the Garvey Movement—an act which would have been futile if the center of his being could not relate to it. I am thinking rather of Langston Hughes's ability to tap the vast reservoir of Blackness in the masses of people, and thereby escape the necessity to feed upon self alone. McKay's person-ality leanings and bondage to Western esthetic tradition are in-volved. Discussing his taste in poetry with Robert Minor, staff member of *The Liberator,* he stated that "my social sentiments were strong, definite and radical, but that I kept them separate from my esthetic emotions, for the two were different and should not be mixed up."[15] Thus we have that peculiar compartmentalization that is so much a part of the central rhythms of Western culture.

In "If We Must Die," the powerful voice of a high-spirited and cultivated black man merges with the rage of his people, and, through its realistic imagery ("hogs," barking of "mad and hungry dogs," etc.) and contemporary relevance replaces the tone of Euro-pean tradition inherent in the sonnet form. In other fine sonnets, McKay is able to make us feel first the note of the black soul, al-though the echo of European tradition may not be entirely sup-pressed. The emotion derives primarily from the black speaker of the poem, secondarily from the plight of his people.

"Baptism," for example, which his autobiography states derives from McKay's experience of being jim crowed in Northern public places, emphasizes the toughness and fineness that the courageous soul derives from having withstood the fire. Paradoxically, sustained and fierce hatred gives vitality and a bitter sweetness to the speaker of "The White City," who is oppressed by the massive symbols of Western machine culture which "Are sweet like wanton loves because I hate."

Among the sonnets which emphasize the individual black speaker, "The White House" stands out for its perfect movement and its suggestiveness regarding the personality responses of the speaker as he opposes his unconquerable soul to the haughty oppression and hypocritical "civilization" symbolized by "The White House." Since the poem cannot be given here the analysis that it merits, I quote the first eight lines to permit it to give its own partial testimony:

> Your door is shut against my tightened face,
> And I am sharp as steel with discontent;
> But I possess the courage and the grace
> To bear my anger proudly and unbent.
> The pavement slabs burn loose beneath my feet,
> A chafing savage, down the decent street;
> And passion rends my vitals as I pass,
> Where boldly shines your shuttered door of glass. . .[16]

Some sonnets contain interesting statements, even when they are somewhat marred by defects. In general, the romantic rebel of 19th Century Romantic tradition hovers nearby some of the best sonnets and threatens to break through the black face. In "America," the poetic speaker expresses ambivalence, loving this "cultured hell that tests my youth," despite its "tiger's tooth" in his throat and the "bread of bitterness" which it feeds him. He stands confidently and casts upon Western arrogance a knowing scrutiny, since he is aware that its "granite wonders" sill sink "Beneath the touch of Time's unerring hand/Like priceless treasures sinking in the sand." The ambivalnce of the speaker is maintained by the concept of the culture as priceless treasures misused.

"America" is somewhat marred because it evokes too literal a recollection of the ending of "Ozymandias," a poem concerning the destruction of a monument to a tyrant, written by the romantic poet Percy Shelley. "Outcast" dramatizes the black speaker's alienation from the rhythms of the Western culture, but contains merely the romantic picture of Africa rendered from time to time by several black Renaissance poets. Its explicit statements are interesting and relevant to current radical feelings concerning "black soul."

44

"Something in me is lost, forever lost/ Some vital thing has gone out of my heart/And I must walk the way of life a ghost/Among the sons of earth, a thing apart. . . ." Although it refers to the Black's condition "Under the white man's menace, out of time," the concluding couplet is more an abstract, intellectual statement, than one which drives the emotions.

"Tiger"· begins dramatically: "The white man is a tiger at my throat. . ." It makes a bitter and ironic commentary on Western assumptions regarding the West as bearer of the "Light," whereas its impact is that of bloodsucker and dollar hustler. But it ends merely in a despairing cry.

It should be seen, however, that in the best of his sonnets, McKay's expression of a powerful, defiant, and embattled black soul, reveals the hand of a master.

It is fitting to end the discussion of sonnets with "The Harlem Dancer," a poem that is both one of McKay's best and the cause of early attention to him. A few images given through the sensibility of the poem's black speaker provide the reader with hints concerning a beautiful and mysterious soul, whose supreme expression of life's wonder and vitality has, except for the speaker, an audience of "wine-flushed boys" and prostitutes. Their interest is in the passion of the moment, the speaker's—in her total self, as he hears her voice "like the sound of blended flutes/Blown by black players upon a picnic day." To him "she seemed a proudly-swaying palm/Grown lovelier for passing through a storm." But "looking at her falsely-smiling face" he "knew her self was not in that strange place."[17] At most, one can perhaps quarrel slightly with the image of "falsely smiling face," which seems a bit heavy-handed when compared with the gentle suggestiveness of the preceding imagery. But the poem moves almost flawlessly—and with a tender, flowing grace. It is an example of how, at his best, McKay could render the illusion of being completely present in the emotion—whether it is toned by tenderness, rage, wonder, or nostalgia.

The best of McKay's poems that are not written in sonnet form are distinguished and lifted by a flowing music. Traditional in form and replete with the attitudes and ceremonies of 19th Century Romanticism, they, nonetheless, establish the poet's more than legal rights to the ground that he tills. Although it is not virgin soil, it is also not barren, and yields poems of frank manly sentiment made worthy of repeated readings by the stoic and together soul from whom their drama and music derive. I refer to such poems as "Flame Heart," "Spring in New Hampshire," "My Mother," "Heritage," and "Memorial."

What McKay frequently needs is the single imposing image or the suggestive phrase that will make the poem an extraordinary experience for the mind. In many poems, the images are without the sharply etched visual outlines that would deepen meaning and distinguish them from their use by other poets. Other flaws: the lame last line, excessive labeling of feelings and emotions, over-simple oppositions of the virtues of the country and the evils of the city. In sum—the poetic concepts, trappings, and ceremonies of 19th Century Romantic tradition, frequently bring a brilliant flight to a sudden and premature end.

But the poet's story emerges, nonetheless, from the body of the poetry. It is the story of a soul whose flight from the village into the machine cultural centers of the West creates a sense of permanent loss. It is conscious now of the disinheritance of all black people, wherever the West has entered with its "wonders," and it can only keep itself together by a sense of its inner rhythms, its occasional glimpses of a warmer world behind, its fleeting loves and fellow-feeling, and its capacity for hatred. In "O World I Love to Sing," McKay cried:

> O World I love to sing! thou art too tender
> For all the passions agitating me;
> For all my bitterness thou art too tender,
> I cannot pour my red soul into thee.

Wallace Thurman in "Negro Poets and Their Poetry" came to a similar conclusion concerning McKay's poetry, noting that "his tragedy" is "that his message was too alive and too big for the form he chose," and that "he could never shape the flames from the fire that blazed within him."[18]

The story of McKay's poetry is also the story of such novels as *Home to Harlem, Banjo,* and *Banana Bottom,* both with respect to the soul's embattlement and the quality of the fiction. In *Home to Harlem,* the soulful way is expressed through Jake, a former longshoreman who has returned to Harlem after deserting an American army intent upon exploiting him as a laborer instead of a fighter

46

against Germans, and Ray, an educated Black whose alienation from both Blacks and Whites blocks him from the uncomplicated celebration of joy that Jake easily achieves. Ray's main function in the novel is to represent a contrast to Jake and to articulate a criticism of Western culture, Jake's to assert an incorruptible innocence while celebrating the joys of the flesh, comradeship, and love. His natural innocence is his salvation, no matter what situation he confronts: the army's attempt to reduce him, living with an English woman who unsuccessfully attempts to keep him tethered, living with a black woman who requires brutality as an ingredient of love, dealing with a labor situation that offers either scabbing or an insincere labor union.

The greatest threat to his sense of innocence derives from the thin plot of the novel. Returning to Harlem, he discovers in Felice, a woman who returns the money he has paid for sexual favors, a natural soulmate. After discovering their natural affinity, Jake loses her for most of the duration of the novel, a fact which allows McKay to explore Harlem joy life. When Jake finds her, she has become the common-law partner of Jake's comrade Zeddy—but has not taken him into the inner citadel of her heart. Zeddy, angered at the threatened loss of Felice, draws a razor, and Jake confronts him with a pistol. Thus the snake has entered the edenic garden of comradeship—but not for long. Both men suffer quick remorse over the threatened corruption of their souls. Zeddy apologizes, and his apology is quickly accepted by Jake. Jake's realization of the threat to his innocence is expressed as follows:

> His love nature was generous and warm without any vestige of the diabolical or sadistic.
> Yet here he was caught in the thing that he despised so thoroughly. . . Brest, London, and his America. Their vivid brutality tortured his imagination. Oh, he was infinitely disgusted with himself to think that he had just been moved by the same savage emotions as those vile, vicious, villainous white men who, like hyenas and rattlers, had fought, murdered, and clawed the entrails out of black men over the common commercial flesh of women.[19]

The form of soul in *Home to Harlem* is really romantic bohemianism. The reader can admire the superiority of Jake and Felice's natural normality, but cannot forget that the real test comes when Jake has given hostages to fortune in the form of a wife and children, a situation in which the vibrations of the black man's condition in Western culture are not so easily brushed aside.

Nevertheless, *Home to Harlem* has fine and memorable scenes, among the best being those involved with the feud between the dining car chef and the pantry man where event and outcome are more sharply realistic. In *Banjo,* the setting for assertion and expression of soul is the waterfront at Marseilles, known as "the ditch," a hangout of prostitutes, pimps, assorted bums, petty thieves, and beachcombers. Banjo is the man of natural soul, who hopes to form an orchestra from the local talent, Ray, again, the critic to articulate the corruption represented by Western culture.

Similar to Jake, Banjo goes through his experiences on the waterfront protected by the inner rhythms of his soul, celebrating the joy and the poetry of his existence through his music, the women attracted to him, and his capacity to relate naturally to all men. Actually, Banjo emerges as a more deeply achieved character than Jake, although he is without a woman to whom he would feel inexorably attached. On the beach, the white men degenerate, but the black men and Banjo, himself, thrive.

> It was as if they were just taking a holiday. They were always in holiday spirit, and if they did not appear to be specially created for that circle, they did not spoil the picture, but brought to it a rich and careless tone that increased its interest. They drank wine to make them lively and not sodden, washed their bodies and their clothes on the breakwater, and sometimes spent panhandled ten-franc notes to buy a second-hand pair of pants.[20]

McKay manages to get into his gallery a variety of portraits and to celebrate African and American black soul. Negroes are seen as never so beautiful "and magical as when they [in dancing] do that gorgeous sublimation of the primitive African sex feeling," which depends "so much on individual rhythm, so little on formal movement," and "is the key to the African rhythm of life." An Arab black girl is described as follows:

Her hair stood up stiff, thick and exciting. Her mouth was like a full-blown bluebell with a bee on its rim, and her eyes were everywhere at once, roving round as only Arab eyes can.[21]

In the interest of soul also are the folk stories of Chapter Ten (although not really woven into the dramatic action), Sister Geter —a black American evangelist, the warm hearted sharing of the beach boys, and soul food. Then there are sufficient attacks verbally upon those who run from their Blackness to delight the heart of any rapper.

Banjo remains, in the end, committed to the vagabond life, and Ray, who is trying to keep together in appropriate rhythm his educated, black and instinctive self, decides that his most promising solution is to cast in his lot with Banjo. "From these boys he could learn how to live—how to exist as a black boy in a white world and rid his consciousness of the used-up hussy of white morality." Thus Ray would retain the innocence of his soul. But, as Banjo points out to Ray, the price of this Edenic existence is a world without women, in any meaningful sense—a kind of chaste homosexual companionship, in which Ray will play a lower-case Huckleberry Finn to Banjo's adapted Nigger Jim. Thus the form of soul becomes a romantic vagabondage.

McKay's criticism of Western pressure upon black soul is often discursive, not a sufficient ingredient in the dramatic structure. But it is very contemporary, except for its inability to recognize that Banjo and Jake are simply moving to another room in a Western prison where their manhood will be no more fulfilled than in the cities that McKay despised. For Ray, the West is the destroyer of all genuine feelings and emotions, of spontaneous gesture, and it is the mechanizer and creator of standardized man. Although a tentative solution is set for the two leading black male characters, Ray, after considering Western modulations of materialism in science-ism, socialism, and communism, still inquires of the machine: "But in this great age of science and super-invention was there any possibility of arresting the thing unless it stopped of its own exhaustion?"

McKay came closer to placing the struggle for the soulful way in the center of culture in his novel *Banana Bottom,* set in Jamaica. Bita, the leading character, is a woman who confronts the problem

Ray has been trying to solve: how to prevent a Western education from separating her from her roots and reducing her soul. Or, in a more positive terms, how to make her Western education work harmoniously with the soulfulness of her roots. In the eyes of the whites who educate her, she is to marry another redeemed Black and help to bring the benefit of Western outlook to her people. Despite being educated in England, Bita is able to resist and to opt for the warmer and spontaneous celebration of life available in the village. McKay, with an abruptness that flaws the dramatic structure of the novel, disposes of the black divinity student whom whites saw as her appropriate mate by having him caught cohabiting with a goat.

After a temporary attachment to Hopping Dick, a celebrator of life's joys but not the marrying kind, Bita resolves her identity crisis by committing herself to the peasant, Jubban. As symbol, of course, the ending works, but it is not a real follow-up of the knotty problem which McKay has laid out. Having had the Western vibrations set up within her, it is unlikely that she could find such an easy resolution in the peasant, Jubban. McKay ends his novel where another problem begins.

The novel's strength resides in McKay's careful attention to re-creating aspects of the folk culture and involves some of his best writing. Unlike the romantic bohemianism of *Home to Harlem* or the romantic vagabondage of *Banjo,* the folk culture, in its way, is called upon to support the total rhythms of existence, and therefore contributes a greater seriousness to *Banana Bottom.*

The problem is that the criticism of the conditions of Blacks in Western culture, and of Western culture, itself, in all three novels places the novels' problems in the category of national significance and demands rather tough-minded answers. On the one hand, Claude McKay works with a more secure grasp of the big picture, the sheer magnitude of the problem of black soul, than did most writers of the Harlem Renaissance, but, on the other, his peculiar sensibility, compounded of his background and sustained commitment to romantic individualism, creates an obstacle course over which his Blackness must run.

I have referred to the initial advantage of McKay's difference in background from most other writers of the Harlem Renaissance—an inheritance of a more positive *niggerhood* that enabled him to coordinate his being quickly for instant powerful expression. In the light of his poetry and fiction, it is possible to see that he was without certain significant resources derived from the situation of American born black writers. The American black folk tradition, for example, had taken its shape from a confrontation with the massive presence of whites, and had had impact upon American born black writers. Thus Langston Hughes, although not born in the deep South, had too intimate a knowledge of the cost of soul to suggest that its celebration could exist outside the edge of a desperation involving such realistic situations as someone's struggling for bread and payment on installments and the rent.

We may compare Hughes's Jimboy of his 1930 novel *Not Without Laughter,* with his counterpart in McKay's novels. The Jimboys involved such mundane matters as empty Christmases and family desertion; therefore, a positing of their innocence could not escape serious reservations. Thus an unqualified celebration of the Jimboys was not really possible for an honest sensibility that understood the situation of blacks under the massive presence and forces of whites. Dues were exacted, and *somebody* paid. In such plays as "Tambourines to Glory" and "Little Ham" Langston Hughes has mechanically set the white world aside, but he is aware of the mechanism and that a simple tug of the strings of the puppet black world will tear down the playhouse of his soul celebraters.

The concept of soul in McKay's poems also tends to be more far-reaching than that reflected in his fiction, which owes something to the white intellectualized concept of black primitivism: unhampered sexual instincts, unstable but sincere emotionality, and relationships between man and woman devoid of persisting tenderness and social values. Such situations would be inapplicable to traditional African societies and to the strong thrusts of individual slaves in America.

How then does McKay continue to speak to your Blackness? I have attempted to indicate that he sets up the ideal of the together soul, one which fits the additional rhythms of the West into its natural patterns. McKay also was aware of the deadly momentum of Western cultural vibrations, even when he seemed to meet it with inadequate resolutions. He anticipated all the stands taken today by those who think of themselves as conscious black men, and understood most deeply than most, as he says directly in the sonnet

51

entitled "The Negro's Friend," that the Black's salvation must come from within.

He, therefore, represents one in a network of individual black men, who made their lives and work and stances a reconnaisance in force prior to the development of a group black consciousness of any magnitude. Like other writers of the Renaissance, he worked with what was at hand, and his achievement represents a *strategic,* rather than a *radical* dissociation of sensibility from that provided by white America and the West. If we can now make that radical dissociation of sensibility, it is because men like Claude McKay went before us.

FOOTNOTES

1. Stephen H. Bronz, *Roots of Negro Racial Consciousness* (New York, 1964), p. 74.
2. James Weldon Johnson, *The Book of American Negro Poetry* (New York, 1931), p. 163. References are to the paperback edition.
3. *Ibid.,* pp. 41, 42. See direct comments upon Paul Laurence Dunbar in Johnson's autobiography, *Along This Way* (New York, 1933).
4. *A Long Way from Home,* p. 24. (References are to 1969 paperback edition.)
5. *A Long Way from Home,* p. 322.
6. Wallace Thurman, *Infants of the Spring* (New York, 1932).
7. Langston Hughes, *The Big Sea* (New York, 1940), pp. 223-335.
8. See Stephen Bronz's analysis of McKay's turn to Catholicism, *Roots of Negro Racial Consciousness,* pp. 88-89.
9. Bronz, p. 85.
10. *A Long Way from Home,* p. 139.
11. *Ibid.,* p. 354.
12. *A Long Way from Home,* p. 354.
13. Compare his quotation from Johnson, *Harlem: Negro Metropolis,* p. 179. Much of the basic conception of Garvey seems influenced by Johnson's. See *Black Manhattan,* pp. 51-59.
14. *A Long Way from Home,* pp. 31-32.
15. *A Long Way from Home,* p. 103.
16. All references and quotations from McKay's poetry are from *Selected Poems of Claude McKay* (New York, 1953). See an interesting analysis of the poem in James A. Emanuel, "The Future of Negro Poetry: A Challenge to the Critics," included in Addison Gayle, Jr., *Black Expression* (New York, 1969), pp. 106-109.
17. For a sense of the atmosphere of the 1920's cabaret scene and the custom of tossing coins to the entertainer, see Ethel Waters's autobiography, *His Eye Is on the Sparrow* (New York, 1951). She also gives an idea of what was required for survival.
18. Wallace Thurman, "Negro Poets and Their Poetry," in Addison Gayle, Jr., editor, *Black Expression,* p. 77.
19. *Home to Harlem* (New York, 1928), p. 173. Reference is to the 1965 paperback edition.
20. *Banjo* (New York, 1929), pp. 18-20.
21. *Ibid.,* pp. 105-106.

Langston Hughes
and
Afro-American Folk
and Cultural Tradition

LANGSTON HUGHES'S LITERARY CAREER BEGAN WITH a commitment to black folk and cultural sources as one important basis for his art. The folk forms and cultural responses were themselves definitions of black life created by Blacks on the bloody and pine-scented Southern soil and upon the blackboard jungle of urban streets, tenement buildings, store-front churches, and dim-lit bars. Thus the current generation of black writers, who are trying to develop artistic forms that reflect a grip upon realities as they exist from day to day in black communities discover that Langston Hughes is an important pioneer, in his non-ideological way, who has already "been there and gone."

From the animal tales to the hipsterish urban myth-making, folk tradition has *is-ness*. Things are. Things are funny, sad, tragic, tragicomic, bitter, sweet, tender, harsh, awe-inspiring, cynical, otherworldly, worldly—sometimes, alternately expressing the conflicting and contradictory qualities; sometimes, expressing conflicting qualities simultaneously. Thus a Brer Rabbit story is full of the contradictions of experience—an expression of the existing order of the world and Brer Rabbit's unspecific sense of something "other." And there are times in Brer Rabbit stories during which the existing order and Brer Rabbit's "other" have almost equal validity.[1]

The black preacher can be a revered personage, but also a figure of comedy, and the oppressed can be sad as victim but comic as a person. As creative artist, Langston Hughes had more of an instinctive, than intellectual, sense of the folk acceptance of the contradictory as something to be borne, climbed on top of, confronted by the shrewd smile, the cynical witticism, the tragicomic scratch of the head, the tense and sucked-in bottom lip, the grim but determined look beyond this life, and, more familiarly, the howl of laughter that blacks have not yet learned to separate from the inanities of minstrel tradition.

Thus, upon entering the universe of Langston Hughes, one leaves at its outer darkness that *type* of *rationality* whose herculean exertions are for absolute resolution of contradictions and external imposition of symmetry. For at many points, though not at all points, Hughes is full of the folk.

And in the face of the stubborn contradictions of life, the folk could frequently call upon their spirits and selves to mount on up a little higher, and simply acknowledge: "It be's that way."

Failure to understand the instance in which the folk do more to move their spirit than to move "objective" reality can lead the critic of the folk and Hughes into a fantasia of misinterpretation. Thus blues critic Samuel Charters in *The Poetry of the Blues* complains because blues singer Bessie Smith's "Long Old Road" expresses great determination to stand up to the terrors of life's journey and to shake hands at journey's end with a friend, but ends in a futility that eliminates the value of the journey: "Found my long lost friend, and I might as well stayed at home."[2] However, Bessie's resolution is in the face-up-to-it-spirit, a tone of pathos, outrage, and defiance mingled, not in the rhetoric of formal rationality.

And thus Robert Bone in his work of criticism, *The Negro Novel in America* (New Haven, 1958) makes neat, clever remarks about ideological confusion in Hughes's novel, *Not Without Laughter,* upon discovering that the story advocates both "compensatory" laughter in the face of life's pain and achievement based upon "the protestant ethic."[3] But expressions such as "the success drive," and "the protestant ethic" simply flatten out into lifeless categories the rich density of the folk hope, which is better expressed by its own terms: "being somebody" and "getting up off your knees." The folk tend to be community oriented; thus in *Not Without Laughter* Aunt Hager and Aunt Harriett (representative of the religious and blues traditions, respectively) tend to see the central character's achievement possibilities in the form of community uplift. It is Aunt Tempy who more nearly represents something that could be called "protestant ethic," and she is rejected. As will be seen later in the essay, the novel does have problems, but it is unlikely that they would be resolved under the neat dichotomies with which Bone deals.

A third major quality that folk tradition reflects in its less self-conscious form is an *as ifness*. Whereas one feels behind self-conscious black literature the unarticulated knowledge that America for Blacks is neither a land of soul nor of bread, a good deal of folklore suggests a complete penetration of its universe, a possession of the land and self in a more thoroughgoing way than that expressed by white American literature. Spirituals, for example, suggest a complete mining of their universe. Many of the animal tales and general folk stories also suggest that a universe has been possessed and defined. The *blues,* however, as a more self-conscious folk form, achieves this confident embracement only in specific songs, since so many of them feature a wanderer and throw such terrible weight upon the individual self. What Langston Hughes and Claude McKay (and possibly Jean Toomer in *Cane*) were able to retain, though sometimes insecurely, were a bounce and warm vitality whose fragile supports are everywhere apparent even when the entire work seems to be devoted to their celebration. The sudden appearance of aggressive symbols of the white world would bring many of the celebrations to a halt or reveal, at least, the high cost of soul. As a result, some black novels end in an otherwise inexplicable romanticism.

Despite the difficulties, Langston Hughes chose to build his vision on the basis of the folk experience as it had occurred in the South and as it appeared modified in the modern industrial city. Judging from his autobiography, *The Big Sea,* his choice proceeded from the center of his being. He liked black folks. He liked their naturalness, their sense of style, their bitter facing up, their individual courage, and the variety of qualities that formed part of his own family background. He was also in recoil from the results of his father's hard choices of exile, hatred of Blacks, self-hatred, and resulting dehumanization. His manifesto of 1926, "The Negro Artist and the Racial Mountain" revealed that choosing the life of the black folk was also a way of choosing himself, a way of possessing himself through the rhythms and traditions of black people. His choice enabled him to allow for prevailing ideologies without being smothered by them, since folk vision could suddenly shift from tenderness to biting cynicism and since within its womb a pragmatic embracement of ideological impulses that promised survival was a secure tradition. Thus, whereas pre-1920's black writers, devoid of a land of soul and a land of bread, found themselves completely at the mercy of that complex of ideas in the social arena known as the American Dream, Hughes brings in aspects of the Dream at will, but so many bitter notes accompany it that he can hardly be said to put much confidence in it. I speak, of course, in the light of the large number of poems that are devoted to other matters. The individual poems, such as "I, Too," which speak of an America that will come to its senses are scattered here and there among poems that discharge the sudden drop of acid. Hughes prized decency in the individual person and could look with compassion upon those corrupted by delusions and systematized prejudice, but in several poems he responded with outrage, bitterness, anger and threat.

It is easily forgotten that one part of "I, Too," speaks of eating well and growing strong, so that no one would *dare* say to the Black, "Eat in the kitchen." In *Selected Poems,* bitterness and desperation are especially apparent in the sections entitled "Magnolia Flowers" and "Name in Uphill Letters," but also directly and indirectly in individual poems among the other sections. In the two sections mentioned, the poems "Roland Hayes Beaten" and "Puzzled" convey the sense of a coming explosion. But one needs merely to range over the body of published poems, in order to sense within Hughes a very powerful ambivalence. Nevertheless, he adopted a psychological approach for his readings to black audiences, described in his second autobiographical book, *I Wonder As I Wander,* an approach which allowed for laughter, then serious and grim situations, and finally the hopeful and stoical stance.[4] Such poems as "I, Too," and "The Negro Mother" gave the positive note without shoving aside the ogres that threatened.

In Langston Hughes's vision, both in regard to the folk and to himself, the most nearly consistent focus is upon a lifesmanship that preserves and celebrates humanity in the face of impossible odds. In regard to himself, Hughes is the most modest of persons. Even his apparent frankness in *The Big Sea* and *I Wonder As I Wander* is deceptive, since his emotional responses are frequently understated or their nuances undramatized. Missing is the close-up focus of the protracted relationship that threatens to reveal the soul or the total person. Thus there are unforgettable pictures—Hughes's relationship to his father and mother, his brief companionship with a refugee girl while down and out in Paris, his conflict with Russian officials over the production of a movie on race relationships in America, etc. But the man behind the picture remains somewhat elusive.

What does emerge is transcendent moments amidst the chaos that society and human nature tend to create. Two or more people getting through to each other, the seizure of richness from surrounding rottenness or confusion, the sudden appearance of the rainbow after the storm, the individual retaining his focus upon the human—the foregoing comprise the stuff of the autobiographies, which are frequently comparable to the episodic experiences of lyrics and convey only the slimmest hint of the single broad meaning that would impose the illusion of unity upon human experience. In all the autobiographical approaches, Hughes is consistent with what I have called the *is-ness* of folk vision and tradition—life is lived from day to day and confronted by plans whose going astray may evoke the face twisted in pain or the mouth open in laughter. The triumph is in holding fast to dreams and maintaining, if only momentarily, the spirit of the self.

As to the folk, Hughes was early captivated by their stubborn lifesmanship. Through his grandmother he had early learned the heroic side of black life, and he had experienced the rituals of the black church and pretended to be saved. As he encountered the urban folk, he was taken in by the full-bodied warmth of their lives, the color, the bounce, the vitality. But he also knew the harshness of their existence in the huge city, since he had spent a summer during adolescence on South State Street in Chicago where his mother was employed by a dress shop. In *The Big Sea: An Autobiography*, he says:

> South State Street was in its glory then, a teeming Negro street with crowded theaters, restaurants, and cabarets. And ex-

citement from noon to noon. Midnight was like day. The street was full of workers and gamblers, prostitutes and pimps, church folks and sinners. The tenements on either side were very congested. For neither love nor money could you find a decent place to live. Profiteers, thugs, and gangsters were coming into their own.[5]

Like Sandy in *Not Without Laughter,* Hughes walked bewildered among the new sights. But the harshness within the black community was not the sum of the situation. When he wandered beyond it, he was beaten by hostile whites.

This early awareness of the embattled situation of folk existence in the Northern city and direct brutality of the Southern life that drove Blacks to urban questing probably protected Hughes from the falsification of folk life that James Weldon Johnson found in the poetry of Paul Laurence Dunbar (see his comments in the two prefaces in *The Book of American Negro Poetry*). Instead of the idyllic, Hughes could portray honestly a people caged within a machine culture, sometimes feeding upon each other, sometimes snarling at the forces without, and sometimes rising above tragedy by the sheer power of human spirit. A people responding to existence through cultural forms and traditions derived from so many terrible years of facing up and demanding, at the same time, a measure of joy and affirmation: the dance, jazz, blues, spirituals, the church. Across the water in France, he found:

> Blues in the rue Pigalle. Black and laughing, heartbreaking blues in the Paris dawn, pounding like a pulse-beat, moving like the Mississippi!

> > *Lawd, I looked and saw a spider*
> > *Goin' up de wall.*
> > *I say, I looked and saw a spider*
> > *Goin' up de wall.*
> > *I said where you goin', Mister Spider?*
> > *I'm goin' to get my ashes hauled!*[6]

The variety of life and its relationship to the self were expressed in simple symbols that allowed for the whole gamut of stances toward existence.

Later, amidst the phoniness that he found in black middle-class Washington society, he was again to encounter the triumphant spirit of the "low-down folks." They served as an inspiration:

> I tried to write poems like the songs they sang on Seventh Street—gay songs, because you had to be gay or die; sad songs, because you couldn't help being sad sometimes. But gay or sad, you kept on living and you kept on going. Their songs—those of Seventh Street—had the pulse beat of the people who keep on going.[7]

Hughes speaks of the "undertow of black music with its rhythm that never betrays you, its strength like the beat of the human heart, its humor, and its rooted power." On Seventh Street, he encountered both the "barrel houses," suppliers of the gay, naughty, and wise music, and the black churches full of song and intense religious experience. It is good to keep in mind the ceremonies of humanity which Hughes found in the folk even when reading of his non-black experiences, since he seems to have sought the same qualities in all people.

The above approach applies to Hughes's writings that are not in folk forms and are not about the folk. He seldom takes up a form that could not express the folk or that expresses *forms of response* to existence that are foreign to their sensibility. This is to say that Hughes was sensitive to the implications of form. Thus he early allied himself with free verse forms. The blues form, with its sudden contrasts, varied repetitions, resolution areas, allows for the brief and intense expression of the ambiguities of life and the self, and for sharp wit and cynicism. The jazz, bebop, and boogie-woogie rhythms achieve a free swing away from Western constraints. One could add comments on the significance of the traditional work songs, the influence of spirituals, shouts, the gospel song, the prayer, the testimonial, and the sermon. Suffice it here to say that they move us into an immediate recognition of a black experience that is at the center of a long tradition, convey attitudes and forms of response to existence, and often give the illusion of confronting us, not merely with lines upon a page, but with a participant of a particular ritual.

Now as James A. Emanuel has ably pointed out in his book, *Langston Hughes*,[8] it is difficult to gain the total blues experience or the musical experience of jazz and other rhythms from the printed page, since the writer is deprived of the embellishments used by the blues singer and the musician. However, the handicap of printed page should alert us to compensations available to the writer, to other dangers that bestride his path, and to Hughes's variation from the standard path of the Western artist. In the first place, it is seldom really of value simply to duplicate a folk form, since the folk artist has already pushed the form to its greatest heights of expressiveness. In mere repetition, the self-conscious artist usually runs the risk of merely echoing achievements that have had the advantage of generations of responsive audiences. His real opportunity is in capturing the spirit of the art, in adapting techniques, in adding to folk forms an articulation of assumptions which the folk artist merely had to hint at because his audience was so closely akin to him (or he was so closely akin to his audience). Thus the self-conscious artist is not necessarily being praised for a very high achievement when the critic points to his creation of a perfect blues or spiritual form.

The above principles regarding the folk artist and the self-conscious writer are true if the printed page is to be the sole basis of judgment, a handicap that Hughes often hurdled by reading his poems directly to audiences (with or without musical accompaniment) and by his close relationship to the black community. He, therefore, to a degree, evaded the confinement to the printed page that is the fate of the alienated or abstracted standard Western artist. Thus he could read the mulatto's statement in the poem "Cross" to an audience that had lived with the white enforced miscegenation that forms the subject of the poem, and deliver a powerful impact. He did not, for example, have to dramatize or explain the changes within the mulatto, who merely states them as conclusions. This kind of compensation, however, was not available for every poem by Hughes, and therefore, he must frequently face the question as to whether he is not operating too close to the folk form.

Any criticism of Hughes must thus also face the instances and the degree to which he varied from the traditional stance of the Western artist. Much of his work is very little reflective of a concern to be *universal* and *timeless*. Instead, the topicality of numerous pieces reflect Hughes's satisfaction in giving the issues of the community an immediate and striking voice.

II

A more concrete demonstration of Hughes's relationship to folk and cultural tradition may be gained from selected fiction, poetry, and drama. Although he became famous during the 1920's as a poet, Hughes reveals the spread of his concerns and their hazards more clearly in literary types that provided considerable sweep, rather than brief lyrical intensity. *Not Without Laughter*, Hughes's first novel, is therefore the starting point, for strategic reasons peculiar to this essay, and its discussion will be followed by an examination of representative poems and plays.

Not Without Laughter portrays a family that is very close to the folk, and reveals styles of confronting the disorder and chaos that attempted to hammer their way into the precariously held sanctuary of black family life. The novel portrays the tensions of a generation that came to adulthood not long after the hopes of Blacks for freedom had been fully brought low throughout the land. (The first reference to time is a letter postmarked June 13, 1912.) The mainstay and would-be shepherd of this generation is Aunt Hager, whose life is an epic of labor over the washtub. Getting ready to meet adulthood as the third generation is her grandson, Sandy, a witness to the perilous hold on life managed by his family: the grandmother; his mother, Anjee; his wandering father, Jimboy; and his aunts, Tempy and Harriett. Although the events controlling the life of each member of the family absorb a goodly portion of the novel, the development and fate of the boy Sandy and especially the extent to which the lives of his elders provide him with a usable resource, form the big question mark in the novel.

Aunt Hager, the grandmother, represents the religious tradition begun in the secret "praise" meetings of slavery and further developed in the little white washed churches that once dotted the countryside and the small towns.

And here we must be aware of the oversimplified versions of black religion, since the race's religious experience, like all other black experiences, requires reevaluation in its own terms, one which

61

will release it from the oversimplified categories of escapism and otherworldliness that were developed by analogy with what is required in duplicating the Faustian quest of whites. Aunt Hager's religion, as Hughes presents it, reflects solemn moments, dogged persistence, and an ability to love and forgive, that gives magnitude to the humblest. It places man against the sky. It allows Aunt Hager, according to her report, to pray for whites that she doesn't like, but she is still pragmatic and unworshipful towards them (unlike Faulkner's Dilsey of *The Sound and the Fury*). In her eyesight, whites, in their relationship with blacks, are good as far as they *see* but they do not see far. This is not to say that Aunt Hager fully grasps or brings into a single focus the hard realities of a racially oppressive system that primarily values her as a work horse and twists the lives of her children into shapes that can grasp joy only by refusing to be stifled by disaster. Since Hughes is aware of her limitations, he counterpoints her determined optimism by the bitter and sinister reports of Jimboy, Sister Johnson, and Harriett, and by portraits of racial injustice.

What impresses Hughes and Sandy is the passionate spiritual power that sustains faith in life and in a day of overcoming. She would like for Sandy to be a Booker Washington and a Frederick Douglass: "I wants him to know all they is to know, so's he can help this black race of our'n to come up and see de light and take they places in de world. I wants him to be a Fred Douglass leadin' de people, that's what, an' not followin' in de tracks of his good-for-nothin' pappy. . . ."[9]

This folk sense of making something out of oneself has a lasting impact upon Sandy, but there are also available to him the jazz and blues tradition through his father Jimboy and his Aunt Harriett. Hughes plays very warmly and lovingly the notes of the tradition that involves a bouncing vitality and a defiant celebration of the sweets, joys, and pains of life, and Sandy finds himself drawn to the people who demand that life yield its more soulful fruits. However, Hughes has a very complex awareness, one that he cannot fully render within the novel. He is also an honest and realistic writer. Therefore, he can not make of Jimboy's situation a very simple triumph and must report the cost of Jimboy's joy, charm, and exhuberance. It is the increased deprivation of his family and some rather painful childhood experiences of Sandy that register the cost of Jimboy's bounce and spontaneity. Thus, despite Hughes's distancing of Jimboy's wide-ranging amours, explanations of the systematic oppression that tends to reduce black men, the portrayal of him as a "rounder" who works and holds good intentions, and dramatization of his ability to transform the atmosphere of his surroundings, Jimboy is never quite clear of the dubious stature which Aunt Hager very early in the novel confers upon him. Jimboy is, after all, *boy*.

Thus the sensitive youth Sandy can only share moments of the tradition represented by his father, can only feel that the swing and bounce that he represents ought, somehow, to be a part of the richness of any life.

Hughes's complex awareness of what the folk were up against in the attempt to assert the free life spirit is also apparent in his portrait of Harriett, who learns through her intermittent bouts with prostitution and utter destitution the price-tag placed by a machine culture upon spontaneity. Near the end of the novel, she seems to be on the way to fame and fortune, but Hughes was too familiar with the instabilities that hovered about the success of the black actors, actresses, and entertainers of this period. For most, it was an up and down sort of life, and the "down" area was often slimy.

Since Aunt Tempy's choice of a bloodless imitation of white society represented for Hughes an obvious surrender of soul, her life represented little that could promise richness to Sandy.

In the end, Sandy is thrown back upon the dreams of Aunt Hager. Although the metaphor seems awkward when applied to her, she too was a dancer of the spirit and held dreams of his becoming the dancer who overshot the unambiguous hazards that, for the folk, skyrocketed the price of soul. Perhaps, one need not literally repeat the folk forms of dancing, the folk existence; perhaps one might achieve fulfillment if one could conceive of Booker Washington and Frederick Douglass as dancers of the spirit, too. Perhaps one could retain much of the folk spirit and attitude as one transformed their dances.

A band of dancers. . . . Black dancers—captured in a white world. . . . Dancers of the spirit, too. Each black dreamer a captured dancer of the spirit. . . . Aunt Hager's dreams for

Sandy dancing far beyond the limitations of their poverty, of their humble station in life, of their dark skins.[10]

Other than folk responses to existence, the novel contains such forms as blues, folk aphrorisms, slave narratives and a slave tall story, dances, and spirituals. Especially significant is the spiritual that comes at the very end, "By an' by when de mawnin' comes. . . ." The spiritual ends with the line, "An' we'll understand it better by an' by!" It tells of overcoming, suggests a determined struggle which cannot be easily conceptualized or understood, and is being sung in the big, raw city of Chicago. As Hughes has said, it is the music of a "people on the go," who are somehow to break free from their cage. The vague aspirations, but settled determination, of Sandy are a fitting part of the ending.

The novel, of course, has its problems. Sandy's consciousness does not develop dramatically, and there are contradictory statements about his degrees of innocence. Jimboy's moral lecture to Sandy comes abruptly, and, seemingly, out of character, and Harriett's insistence upon the vision of Aunt Hager needs stronger foreshadowing. Finally, the ending does not dramatically impose itself upon the reader, although it is logically the right one. Much of the source of the foregoing deficiencies seems to be Hughes's complex awareness of the hard and stubborn realities, which the characters will somehow have to overcome. He is almost too aware of the uncertanties of black life.

On the other hand, the novel makes clear the sensibility that created the poems which preceded it and followed it, and looks forward to the rough urban responses provided by his short stories, the simple sketches, and the plays. For *Not Without Laughter* emphasizes Hughes's awareness of the overwhelming oppression that dancers of the spirit faced in both rural and urban cages of the American machine culture, the limitations in the major forms of folk culture, and the increasing difficulty of asserting the triumph of the spirit, as will be reflected by the poems and plays that form the remainder of this discussion.

In his essay, "The Harlem of Langston Hughes' Poetry," in *Phylon,* Arthur P. Davis has cogently pointed out the increasing desperation and the decreasing emphasis upon joy in poems devoted to urban Harlem reflected in the major collections of poetry from

The Weary Blues through *Montage of a Dream Deferred.*[11] The volumes represent the adaption of the folk spirit to the big urban surroundings, and the attempt to transform the threatening pressures of city machine culture into a poetry responsive to the spirit and often to transcend by defiant assertion of spirit. On the one hand are the tough and soulful blues, the cabarets and jazz bands, the singers, and sparkling personalities; on the other, the stark up-creep of weariness and the varieties of offenses to the human spirit unleashed by the city. To these may be added other urban poems that do not deal with Harlem, the more rural Southern poems, or poems on the general theme of the South, and poems on the general theme of the qualities and dilemmas of Blacks. Finally, there are the poems that address themselves to life, without regard to race. The variety of categories makes possible a variety of notes and attitudes.

Hughes's most obvious and original innovation was the introduction of blues form and attitudes as part of the art of poetry as pointed out by Margaret Walker.[12] The use of such blues devices as swift contrasts, sharp wit, voice tones, and folk imagery, frequently create striking effects, despite the lack of musical accompainment and gesture that were available to the blues singer. "Midwinter Blues" which first appeared in *Fine Clothes to the Jew,* seems to me to catch the essential folk spirit adapted to an urban setting and to contain the literary possibilities of the form. The poem taken from *Selected Poems of Langston Hughes* begins:

> In the middle of the winter,
> Snow all over the ground.
> In the middle of the winter,
> Snow all over the ground—
> 'Twas the night befo' Christmas
> My good man turned me down.

The conjunction of the cold of the winter with the associations we have with Christmas and the contrasting actual response of "my good man" get the poem off to an incisive start and combine narrative and blues techniques. However, the second stanza has the sudden turn of wit and irony of attitude more closely associated with the blues.

---

* In *Langston Hughes: Black Genius.* Thurman B. O. Daniels,, ed. (New York, 1971)

Don't know's I'd mind his goin'
But he left me when the coal was low.
Don't know's I'd mind his goin'
But he left when the coal was low.
Now, if a man loves a woman
That ain't no time to go.

The third and fourth stanzas, unfortunately, lack the power of the first two, but the third stanza does bring in a new response of the *contradictory self*. Despite the somewhat snide remarks in the first two lines of the second stanza, the "good man" is acknowledged as "the only man I'll/Love till the day I die." The fourth stanza states a general attitude that requires the voice of the blues singer to maintain intensity and to assert the toughness of spirit characteristic of the blues. Frequently, the last stanza seems to lose intensity, simply because we do not have the ingenious use of triumphant tone that the actual blues singer is able to render.

Thus "Young Gal's Blues" has three closely knit stanzas by written literary standards. The fourth is related to the other three in an associational way, but an actual blues singer would bring home both its power and relatedness. On the other hand, "Down and Out," which first appeared in *Shakespeare in Harlem*, 1942, maintains its unity, sings itself, and provides an interesting effect by an *apparently* anti-climactic arrangement and the repetition of the last line.

Baby, if you love me
Help me when I'm down and out.
If you love me, baby,
Help me when I'm down and out,
I'm a po' gal
Nobody gives a damn about.

The credit man's done took ma clothes
And rent time's nearly here.
I'd like to buy a straightenin' comb,
An' I need a dime fo' beer.

I need a dime fo' beer.

As a song, "Down and Out" would lend itself to a variety of singing styles. As a written work, the concision of the first verse and the suggestiveness regarding the blues attitudes in the second verse allow for the activity of the creative reader. Several poems provide both this unity and suggestiveness: "Lament Over Love," "Stony Lonesome," Miss Blues'es Child," and "Hard Daddy," for example. Obvious literary unity, however, does not always produce the powerfully expressed folk spirit, since, in its own style, the poem must compete with the folk blues poem whose black audiences hold assumptions in common with the singer—a fact that permits him to impose a unity not based upon simple logical structure but upon his total performance. The following lines by Blind Lemon Jefferson as I have been able to gather them from Samuel Charters' edited record, *The Country Blues,* will illustrate the non-logical structure with which the blues singer is free to operate. Jefferson gives it a powerful rendering by his damn-my-hard-luck-soul variations in tone:

> I'm gwine to de river
> Walk down by the sea (Repeated)
> I got those tadpoles and minnows
> Arguing over me.
>
> Settin' here wonderin'
> Will a match-box hold my clothes (Repeated)
> Ain't got so many matches
> But I got so far to go.
>
> Lord, mama, who may your manager be?
> Hey, hey, mama, who may your manager be?
> You ask so many questions, can't you
> Make 'rangements for me?
>
> I got a girl way cross town
> She crochet all the time (Repeated)
> Baby, if you don't stop crocheting
> You goin' lose your mind.
>
> I wouldn't mind marrying,
> But I can't stand settlin' down
> Wouldn't mind marryin'
> But, Lord, settlin' down
> I'm goin' act like a preacher

An' ride from town to town.

I'm leaving town
Cryin' won't make me stay,
I'm leavin' town, woo-oo
Cryin' won't make me stay,
The more you cry, baby,
The more you drive me away.

The blues lyric has behind it enough audience assumptions regarding the singer's message to make a discussion for a separate essay: the gritty circumstances that inform the mood; the appearance of the prostitute in the third stanza; the implications concerning the girlfriend in the fourth stanza "crocheting" (sexual intercourse); views of marriage and the preacher; attitudes of lovers; the character of the roving "rounder," etc. I leave the analysis of imagery, the associational development, and *apparent* difficulty of the images of the *river* and the sea, to the reader.

My point is that the conscious literary artist runs the risk of appearing second-rate when he is compared with the blues artist at his best, if he simply tries to mine exactly the same ore. In the "Match-Box Blues," the challenge resides even in the blues poem as literary lyric, since its images and associational development allow it to penetrate so suggestively the privacy and complexity of a particular black experience. (This associational development is greatly admired when it appears in a poem by T. S. Eliot). It is perhaps not too much to say that even on a purely literary basis Hughes has trouble matching the authority wielded here by Blind Lemon Jefferson, in the poems that follow strictly the validated blues form.

I would tentatively say that Hughes is best when he attempts to capture the blues spirit and varied forms of response to existence in a poem that uses non-blues devices. Among such poems would be "Reverie on the Harlem River," "Early Evening Quarrel," "Mama and Daughter," and especially, "Lover's Return." Such poems can combine the simplicities of free verse, the free dramatizing of concrete situations, the folk tendency to hold in suspension contradictory attitudes, the incisive folk definition, and various formal resources of literary technique, for the effective rendering that is more available to the self-conscious and relatively isolated artist.

In an overall way, it may also be said that Hughes gains a good deal from experimentation with blues form. One certainly could not imagine his having to buy a Bessie Smith record, as James Baldwin reports that he once did, in order to get back to how Blacks actually express themselves or to recapture the sound patterns of their speech. Hughes seldom strikes a false note with black sound patterns, and these are apparent also in non-blues poems. His poems are also full of the hard complex attitudes of the people stubbornly "on the go," whom he mentions in his autobiography, *The Big Sea.* He is seldom at the mercy of forms that immediately evoke experiences whose essentials are not those of the black experience, a dilemma that sometimes catches up with Claude McKay as we hear him crowded by the romantic tradition and the sudden notes of Byron or Shelley.

It is, of course, possible to credit too much to his contact with a single form, and to overlook the fact that Hughes was drawing from the whole of black culture. Suffice it to say that the self confronting defiantly the enemy at home and abroad is amply evident in his blues and blues toned poems.

There is evidence in Hughes's poetry of his capturing the forms of response of the folk implied by the religious tradition and its cultural modes of expression: the spirituals, gospel songs, and the sermon. In most of such poems the concentration is not on the close duplication of form that is sometimes encountered in the blues poems, but upon mood, definitions, motifs, and the determination and persistence provided by having a friend not made of earth. Such approaches to life can sometimes be rendered through dramatization of personalities who sometimes mention God—but not always. Such poems as "Aunt Sue's Stories," "The Negro Mother," "Mother to Son," and even the poem that strikes the blues note, "Stoney Lonesome," convey a sense of standing erect upon the earth by means of a quiet but deep relationship to something more than this world.

Perhaps the closest that Hughes came to attempting to catch the immediate bounce and beat of a form is the emphasis upon the gospel music form and beat found in the poem, "Fire," which begins:

> Fire,
> Fire, Lord!
> Fire gonna burn ma soul!

The beat of the gospel music can be heard, and if one has been exposed to the musical accompaniment, it too can be heard. But it is only necessary to read a few gospel songs or to hear Mahalia Jackson render one in the ecstatic modulations that have made her famous to realize that Hughes is trying neither to mount to the heights or to give the typical resolution of conflict that is usually essential to the form. In the spiritual tradition, Hughes is better at rendering the quieter moments, even when they involve desperation, which may be found in such poems as "Sinner," "Litany," "Feet of Jesus," and "Judgment Day," although he can mount to the ecstatic by combining well established lines and images drawn from tradition with other literary resources as he does in "Spirituals."

Hughes's spectacular effort in the vein of the folk sermon is "Sunday Morning Prophecy," but he makes no effort to exploit the full sermon form: the conventional apology for ineptitude, the clear statement and explanation of text, and the movement into ecstatic seizure by the spirit. The ecstatic seizure and eloquent imagery characteristic of the folk sermon are utilized, but the emphasis is finally upon the powerful condemnation of things of this world and the minister's final plea:

> Come into the church this morning,
> Brothers and Sisters,
> And be saved—
> And give freely
> In the collection basket
> That I who am thy shepherd
> Might live.
> Amen!

The associations that people have with the urbanized folk minister of Cadillac fame can raise issues concerning the interpretation of the poem, if one is also acquainted with the rural or small town folk minister who was expected by the congregation to make the same plea for his meager remuneration. If Hughes is thinking of the Cadillac preacher, then the effect is irony, but somewhat grotesque and the means seem out of proportion to the effect. It seems more effective to consider the poem in line with the folk tendency to balance apparent contradiction without feeling the urge for logical symmetry.

More important for Hughes is his sense of the power to persist, and perhaps eventually to prevail, which the religious impulse and definitions provide. To persist, that is, with human personality and its full range, refusing to be destroyed and determined to overcome "some day." Here Hughes is dealing with a cultural dimension that deeply reflects the desperate history of a people caged in a machine culture. It is, in its urban setting, in accord with the ending of the novel *Not Without Laughter,* in which Sandy finds in Chicago his people hard embattled but retaining that dance of the spirit which they insisted upon amidst the ravages of slavery. In the poetry of Hughes, the dance moves sometimes in a deeply contemplative slow drag, sometimes in the fast triumphal pace inescapable in gospel music.

In a modified folk tradition also are poems which fit into no particular category, but represent depths of lives, nonetheless. "Railroad Avenue" celebrates the transforming power and spirit of laughter; "Me and the Mule" expresses stubborn self-acceptance and defiance; and "Mama and Daughter," the male-female attraction and resentment. Other poems touch upon a wide range of topics: defiance in the face of discrimination, the potential sudden explosion of put-upon people, the African heritage, the on-the-go impulse in the face of oppression, police brutality, etc. And still others range over topics that cannot be said to have a direct relation to folk and cultural tradition.

Finally, there are the published plays, some of which yield their full depths only when related to folk and cultural tradition.[13] The play version of "Mulatto" is a tragedy, whose title suggests a focus upon the mulatto Robert, the son of the white Georgia plantation owner Colonel Norwood and his black housekeeper, Cora. However, the deeper aspects of the play derive from Cora and the narrow range of choices within which the plantation folk have had to make their definition of the possibilities of life. After submitting to sexual advances by Norwood in a seduction involving both her fear and attraction, Cora, at the age of fifteen, received her plantation mother's definition of her situation:

> Then I cried and cried and told ma mother about it, but she didn't take it hard like I thought she'd take it. She said fine white mens like de young Colonel always took good care o' their

colored womens. She said it was better than marryin' some black field hand and workin' all your life in de cotton and cane. Better even than havin' a job lik ma had, takin' care o' de white chilluns.[14]

Within this narrow margin of something "better," Cora has tried to move her relationship with Norwood from that of simple sexual exploitation into one in which natural claims of fatherhood and motherhood could prevail. Norwood has been married, but Cora is the sole source of his fatherhood, his only resource for rising above the mere category of *whiteness*. Cora's deepest pride is in the potential magnitude of her role. Otherwise, she has to be content with the fact that by force of personality she has compelled Norwood to educate his children, an act that strains and goes beyond the customary code governing miscegenation in the Georgia county. Thus, on the one hand Norwood strains the white code until it and its compulsions overtake him; on the other, Cora has strained the folk code, which only promised, in the definition provided by her mother, relief from brute labor. The clash between the claims of whiteness and the claims of the rhythms of natural fatherhood produces Norwood's tragedy: in the final analysis, he cannot exist without the validation of whiteness, a situation expressed by his participation in a lynching and the remorseful aftermath, his beating of his son for publicly calling him father, and the line he draws between Cora and himself: "There was no touchin' Bert, just like there was no touchin' you [Norwood]. I could only love him, like I loved you." The situation collapses completely as the mulatto son Robert chokes his father to death and then destroys himself to prevent being lynched by the mob. Robert acted after Norwood had drawn a pistol, in an attempt to force Robert to act, not like the son he demanded to be, but like a plantation darky.

The one-act play "Soul Gone Home" presents a mother crushed by the pressures of the city and self-betrayals, one result of which is the death of her illegitimate son from undernourishment and tuberculosis. By allowing the dead son and the mother to argue the essential realities of their lives, Hughes breaks through the simple realistic form which would merely have rendered a picture of environmental determinism. The reader is kept off balance, since no simple categories will sum up the density of the folk reality in the urban city as rendered by the dramatic structure. The folk element may be summed up by the compulsions of the mother: the emphasis upon all aspects of the decorum demanded by death—passionate mourning, the proper appearance of the dead, the set role of the bereaved mother, and the motif of the uneasy and troubled spirit. Within this frame, we learn, unsentimentally, of the tragedy of the mother, who has been reduced to prostitution in her effort to survive, and that of the boy—both the child to whom she, in her own way, has been attached and partially the premature instrument of her efforts to survive.

The remaining published plays in *Five Plays by Langston Hughes* are comedies which deserve more comment than can here be given to them. "Little Ham," "Tambourines to Glory," and "Simply Heavenly" all have their settings in Harlem.

The world of "Little Ham" is a bit beyond the folk, but involves cultural traditions and adaptations: the hipster, the actress who engages in high-level prostitution, the numbers men, the operators of shoe-shine and beauty parlors, and the promoters of the latest dances. Hughes is interested in what his smart personalities retain from the blues and jazz traditions: the fierce vitality, the insistent celebration of joy, and the frank and skilled seizing upon the fruits of existence. Laughter. Hughes gives effective rendering to those qualities by allowing nothing to become too serious: guns are drawn but do not kill, women begin to fight but do not maim, a disgruntled lover is comically locked away, and two-timing mates cast new and warm glances upon each other. Then, too, the pressures of the white world are cooled out before being released. One does not, however, escape entirely the awareness that a few touches of hard realism would turn the celebrators into sullen puppets of the gangsters and corrupt police who control the fat that permits the celebration. The play, nonetheless, has power and charm.

In the play, "Tambourines to Glory," Hughes again keeps the white world on the periphery while he unites the traditions of the blues and the spirituals in the struggles of Laura and Essie, who, from different motives become religious evangelists. Laura requires money and the presence of a flesh and blood comforter right here on earth, who can minister to her loneliness. She engages in a struggle to control the affections of Big-Eyed Buddy Lomax, a pimp-like figure with contacts that reach into the underworld. In the course of her losing struggles, she evokes the man-woman struggle that harks back to the folk ballads and folklore. Her struggle finally ends in her murdering Lomax, since her bouncing energy does not provide her with the power over the rampaging male that she admired in her North Carolina mother. Essie, on the other hand, triumphs through a simple Christian love and her desire to uplift the people. She is able also to bring forward representatives of a newer generation with brighter hopes and dreams. The play is filled with gospel songs, spirituals, folk and hipsterish definitions.

In a quieter vein, Simple of "Simply Heavenly," more famous as the Southern migrant and curbstone philosopher of Hughes's sketches, manages finally to get his divorce from his first wife and prepares to marry his church-going, respectable girl-friend, Joyce. The play is filled with the varieties of song and character. Simple does not have quite the salty wit that he displays in the sketches, but retains his character as Hughes's ordinary black man with uncommon common sense and perception.

The works discussed offer a wide range of the manner and methods of Langston Hughes with black folk and cultural tradition, and they reflect a good deal of his achievement as a writer. It is difficult to imagine having to conceive both the battles and the joys of black life without him. His great value is in the range of notes that he was able to play regarding the souls and strivings of black folks. Moving so frequently with a strong sense of definitions and responses derived from the intense struggles that cryptically flash from folk and cultural traditions, his representations of black life usually carry the ring of the true metal, whether he is responding to the topic of the day or trying to reach deeply into the heart of being. His gift was also to catch the shifting tones of the times and to sense the continuity of old things among the new. Thus he always seems current with the newer forces that arise with each decade. Like the folk in their assertion of spirit over circumstance, he usually gives the impression of being "on top of it," an achievement that actually came from constant experimentation and work.

Now it is a commonplace that Hughes is uneven. I have suggested that a part of this "unevenness" derives from his lack of the concentrated Western concern about the immortality of the writer and his works. Hughes was often the social poet, committed to the tasks of the time. Perhaps a more serious criticism is that his awareness on many occasions seems more complex than the art which he can command to render it. His works in the folk area remain closer to the folk definitions in their original form than the self-conscious artist can afford to be, since he lacks the folk artist's well-defined audience. The consequence is that we look in vain for a few works that radiate with the big vision. On the other hand, it is apparent today that he almost always worked the right ground and broke and tilled it. So that today those who follow will find a field clearly marked out and in readiness for deeper harvesting.

FOOTNOTES

1. See especially "Brer Rabbit and Sis Cow" and "Why Brer Rabbit Wears a 'Round-'bout" in Langston Hughes and Arna Bontemps, *The Book of Negro Folklore* (New York, 1958) pp. 4-6. In this discussion of folk-lore and folk tradition, I have been particularly influenced by Ralph Ellison, *Shadow and Act* (New York, 1954),, and by discussions with my colleague, Professor Charles Long, Divinity School, University of Chicago.
2. *Poetry of the Blues* (New York, 1963), p. 33.
3. *The Negro Novel in America* (New Haven, 1965), p. 77.
4. *I Wander as I Wander* (New York, 1956), pp. 55-60.
5. *The Big Sea* (New York, 1940), p. 33.
6. *Ibid.,* pp. 162-163.
7. *Ibid.,* pp. 208-210.
8. James A. Emanuel, *Langston Hughes* (New York, 1967), pp. 137-146.
9. *Not Without Laughter* (New York, 1930), p. 146.
10. *Ibid.,* p. 313.
11. *Phylon*, XIII (Fourth Quarter, 1952), pp. 276-283.
12. Margaret Walker, "New Poets," in Addison Gayle, Jr., ed., *Black Expression* (New York, 1969), p. 97.
13. Webster Smalley, ed., *Five Plays by Langston Hughes* (Bloomington, Indiana, 1963).
14. *Ibid.,* p. 32.

Richard Wright:
Blackness
and
the Adventure
of Western Culture

I SHALL TRY TO FOCUS UPON THREE SOURCES OF Wright's power: his double-consciousness, his personal tension, and his dramatic articulation of black and white culture.

His double-consciousness and personal tension can be discussed at the same time, since one flows into and activates the other. His personal tension springs from a stubborn self conscious of victimization but obsessed with its right to a full engagement of universal forces and to a reaping of the fruits due from the engagement. This right may be called the heritage of Man. And *double-consciousness* —W. E. B. DuBois, in *The Souls of Black Folk,* described it as the black's sense of being something defined and imprisoned by the myths of whites and at war with his consciousness of American citizenship—his heir-apparency to the potentials announced by the so-called period of Enlightenment. The consciousness of American citizenship lights aspiration, but impels the artist to look worshipfully upon the general American culture, and to devalue his condition and that of his people, even when he is conscious of their beauty:

> The innate love of harmony and beauty that set the ruder
> souls of his people a-dancing and a-singing raised but confusion

Reprinted from *C L A Journal,* XII, No. 4, June, 1969.

and doubt in the soul of the black artist; for the beauty revealed to him was the soul beauty of a race which his larger audience despised, and he could not articulate the message of another people.[1]

Frantz Fanon, in *Black Skins, White Masks,* says simply that the Black is over-determined from without, and gives this dramatic picture: "I progress by crawling. And already I am being dissected under white eyes, the only real eyes."[2] In literature, the war of two consciousness sometimes drives for an art that is "only incidentally" about Negroes, if it is about them at all; in which case the writer carefully reduces his particularism (the tensioned details of the black experience) and hustles to the "universal" (usually the culturally conditioned Western version). Other choices: to portray the exoticism that satisfies the symbolic needs of whites; to plead the humanity of blacks before a white audience; and, lately, to dig out and address a black audience, regarding its condition and its beauty. Within the concept of double-consciousness, it will be seen that Wright was both the cunning artificer and the victim.

But first, his personal tension, without which he may not have created at all, a tension, not really separable from the double-consciousness, that is one great source of his creative power. A slight handicap here, from the angle of scholarly documentation. The main source for information concerning Wright's early youth is still *Black Boy,* a great autobiography, but one whose claim to attention is the truth of the artist, and not that of the factual reporter. Both Ralph Ellison and Constance Webb, Wright's biographer, have identified incidents which Wright did not personally experience, incidents from folk tradition.[3] I see no great to-do to be made over Wright's artistic license, since folk tradition is the means by which a group expresses its deepest truths. Thus the picture, if not all the pieces, is essentially true.

What *Black Boy* reveals is that more than any other major black writer, Wright, in his youth, was close to the black masses—and in the racially most repressive state in the union, Mississippi. Worse still, Wright received violent suppression without the easement provided by the moral bewilderment and escapism so available in black culture. Such institutionalized instruments of bewilderment as the otherworldly religion, the smiling side of the "good" white folks, sex, liquor, and the warmth of the folk culture, formed no sustaining portion of his psychic resources. Parents, whose complicity in oppression made for physical security in the South of the pre-and post-World War I periods, were ineffectual. Wright's father was a zero. His mother—a woman bearing up under tensions from the terrors of the daily world, abandonment by a shiftless husband, and painful and disabling sickness—was hard-pressed by Wright and her own tough-minded honesty. Under a persistent barrage of questions concerning black life, answers escaped her lips that merely confirmed the boy's sense of embattlement in a world of naked terror; first, for example, explaining that a white man did not whip a black boy because the black boy was his son, she then sharpened a distinction: "The 'white' man did not *whip* the 'black' boy. He *beat* the 'black' boy."[4]

Constance Webb states Wright's conscious purpose: "To use himself as a symbol of all the brutality and cruelty wreaked upon the black man by the Southern environment."[5] By depressing his middle class background, Miss Webb continues, he would create a childhood that would be representative of most Negroes. Both the power of the autobiagraphy and its flaws develop from Wright's single-minded intention. Actually, for much of the work, his strategy is to posit a self-beyond-culture—that is, the self as biological fact, a very tough biological fact, indeed. A cosmic self, which reaches out naturally (though in twisted and violent patterns) for the beauty and nobleness of life. The self is battered by the white racist culture, and, for the most part, by a survival-oriented black culture, that counters the impulse to rebelliousness and individuality by puritanical repressiveness, escapism, and base submission. That is, black culture suppressed the individual, in order to protect the group from white assault. The dramatic rendering of these forces and the stubborn persistence of the outsider self comprise the major strategy of the book.

And out of that strategy comes an overwhelming impact. Tension, raw violence and impending violence, which evoke, psychologically, a nightmare world in the light of day. The autobiography's first great subject is the growth of consciousness, the stages of which are communicated by statements of the reactions of self to preceding events. In confronting a racist America the black boy's consciousness learns to hide its responses and to pursue its aspirations by secret means. It is damaged for life, but it has avoided becoming a natural product of the system: the stunted, degraded, shuffling Black, almost convinced of its own inferiority and the god-like power of whites. In the latter part of the book, through reading rebellious books, the consciousness of that other self—the white-defined Negro-victim—loses ground to the consciousness of self as American: the heir to the energy releasing resources of the Enlightenment. A desperate hope is created.

Thus *Black Boy's* second great subject: the disinherited attempting to reclaim the heritage of Modern Man.

Black Boy is a great social document, but it could easily have been greater. Its simple naturalistic form, knocks the reader off balance, but then comes reflection. Its universe of terror is little relieved by those moments of joy that usually glide like silent ancestral spirits into the grimmest childhood. To account artistically for the simple survival of the narrator is difficult. Except for the "cultural transfusion" that the narrator receives near the end, Wright gives little artistic emphasis to cultural supports. The careful reader will pick up, here and there, scattered clues. For example, the extended family, with all its short-comings, show a desperate energy and loyalty. Reading was an early feeder of his imaginative life, and the role of his mother in supplying imaginative and emotional help was crucial. In *Black Boy,* the dramatic form does not, in itself, give her a decisive role, but the beatings, teasings, grim love and sporadic periods of silent understanding, imply an unorthodox devotion. The narrator reveals something of the sort in stating the impact of her sickness upon him:

> Already there had crept into her speech a halting, lisping quality that, though I did not know it, was the shadow of her future. I was more conscious of my mother now than I had ever been and I was already able to feel what being completely without her would mean.[6]

There were important facets of ordinary black life, which Wright did not understand because he saw them as an outsider or from the point of view of embattled adolescence. His father was simply the peasant-victim, with a life shaped by the rhythms of the seasons—a classification very likely to have been derived from his Marxian studies. In Memphis, Wright (or the narrator) meets Mrs. Moss, a spontaneously warm and generous black woman, with an equally warm and spontaneous daughter, Bess. Bess likes Richard and, in no time flat, wishes to marry him. The narrator is aware of her qualities, but ascribes their source to what he was later to understand as "the peasant mentality."

Yet this warm spontaneity, as much as the warped puritanism of his own environment, was a value bulwarked and preserved by the embattled black cultural tradition—not by nature or the rhythm of the seasons. Thus the utter bleakness of black life, its lack of tenderness, love, honor, genuine passion, etc., which Wright in a now famous passage in the second chapter of the autobiography noted as general characteristics, were partly reflections of his immediate home life and surroundings: "I had come from a home where feelings were never expressed, except in rage or religious dread, where each member of the household lived locked in his own dark world, and the light that shone out of this child's heart [Bess's] . . . blinded me."[7]

Personal tension and the double-consciousness. In response to white definitions, Wright was able to say to whites that he formed an equation not known in their definitions. Regarding his people, he was able to say that they are much like you define them but you, and not Nature, are responsible. If today, this no longer seems enough to say, or even to be free of a certain adolescent narcissism, we can at least concentrate upon what insights should have been available to Wright during his time. If Wright in *Black Boy* seems too much concerned with warfare upon white definitions, it is good to remember that our growing ability to ignore them exists because the single-minded assault of Wright and others shook up the confidence of a nation and impaired their efficiency.

What can be held against him is that he seemed to have had little awareness that black life, on its own terms, has also the measure of beauty and grandeur granted those who are often defeated but not destroyed. It would be good here to know more about his reading, especially works written by black men. How startling, for example, to learn from Constance Webb that at the age of thirty-two, in 1940, Wright had not read Booker T. Washington's *Up from Slavery*. In a footnote to Chapter 13 of *Richard Wright,* Miss Webb states:

Wright was almost ashamed to admit that he had never read *Up from Slavery*. He had escaped being educated in Negro institutions and never got around to reading those books which everyone was supposed to read. He did know that the greatest split among educated Negroes of a generation or so ago was over Washington's proposals.[8]

Miss Webb is valiant, but the explanation is lame. That very boyhood which Wright was attempting to understand in *Black Boy* depends, for proper dimension, upon an intimate knowledge of Booker T. Washington and W. E. B. DuBois and of the issues with which they grappled. Ironically, by 1903, DuBois in "Of Our Spiritual Strivings," *The Souls of Black Folk*, had already defined the problems and the danger which Wright (born in 1908) would confront as a writer.[9] Aside from such considerations, it would hardly seem that a person as obsessed with black problems as Wright was would require an education in Negro institutions to put him in touch with the major figures in his history.

The truth is probably that having caught a breath of life from the literature of revolt against the American small town and from Marxian dialectics Wright was over impressed with their efficiency as tools to explore the privacy and complexity of the black environment. Certainly, Ellison, in 1941, described a system that Wright used for mastering culture that was double-edged and required wariness. Ellison praised Wright for translating the American responses that he heard whites express into terms with which to express the life of Bigger Thomas in *Native Son*. Ellison credited Wright with thus building up within himself "tensions and disciplines . . . impossible within the relaxed, semi-peasant environs of American Negro life."[10] Now such a system can immediately broaden and deepen perspective, but it also carries an obvious payload of distortion. In this regard, it is interesting to note that Ellison, who, in 1945, was obviously disturbed by Wright's famous description of black life as bleak and barren, now says that it is simply a paraphrase of Henry James's description in his *Hawthorne*, of "those items of high civilization which were absent from American life during Hawthorne's day, and which seemed so necessary in order for the novelist to function."[11] One might add that the hard and sharp articulate terms of the black narrator's individualism and rationalism in *Black Boy* seem occasionally to be imports from Northern urban middle-class culture. Neither the folk black culture of the 1920's nor the general Southern culture allowed a childhood to escape the compulsion toward an almost superstitious display of forms of reverence for its elders—even when "reality" gave no justification for them. The rebellion against such a compulsion would, if natively expressed, have been less confident and articulate, more in the forms of silence, sullenness, and guilty outbursts.

In *Black Boy*, the young Richard Wright's impulse to individuality has already begun to engage the dominant forms of Western culture. It promises arms for the freedom of both the black artist and his people. On the other hand, the forms have, for him, their dead-end streets. Individualism in Western culture ranges from rugged activity to imprisonment in one's own subjectivity. While enabling one to escape the confines of a survival-oriented folk culture and to take arms against the West's racism, Western cultural forms threaten to subtly transform the emotional and psychic reflexes, so that while the black writer's status is one of alienation, his deepest consciousness is that of the exaggerated Westerner.

In successive autobiographical statements Wright's alienation was apparent. In "The Man Who Went to Chicago,"[12] the picture is one of alienated man trying to express impulses which the forms of Western culture are supposedly dedicated to promoting: the triumph of the human individual (as Fanon termed it), of curiosity, and of beauty. But in Chicago, the capitalistic culture was giving no public sanction to the possession of such qualities by black men, and "adjusted" blacks were themselves an obstacle, as they vied for status in their misery.

Within the Communist Party, as reflected in "I Tried to Be a Communist," Wright found the "triumph of the human individual" balked on ideological grounds.[13] As to the racial thing, one leftist writer confessed, while recruiting Wright, for a Communist front group, that "We write articles about Negroes, but we never see any Negroes."[14] When it came to getting Wright a room in the New York City of 1935, the Communists went through the same foot-shuffling affected by other white Americans, and, in order to attend the Communist-sponsored conference, Wright, himself, found a room in the Negro Y.M.C.A., miles from the site of the conference.

Wright, a very big man, was aware that the Communists had no understanding of the depths of the lives of black men. But Marxism was *the* dynamic philosophy for social change. Where else was he to go? Meanwhile, his life reflected, in an eighth grade dropout's mastery of world culture, the great Western ideal: the expression of the individual life as revolutionary will. The process jerked uptight his emotional and moral reflexes. When he confronted African culture in *Black Power* or met representatives of non-Western cultures, he was both the alienated black man and the exaggerated Westerner, and was at once sympathetic and guiltily sniffy.[15] The fit of the two is uneasy. In *Black Power, Pagan Spain, The Color Curtain,* and *White Man, Listen!,* non-fictional works, the personality behind the print ranges from that of a bright, but somewhat snippish Western tourist to that of a Western schoolmarm, although his ideas are most frequently interesting and provocative.

But Wright remained embattled

And in the 1950's, in the novel *The Outsider,* he was raising the question as to whether the Western game had not lost all vitality.

II

For Richard Wright the job of writing was most serious and his struggle was very great. In "Blue-Print for Negro Writing," he saw blacks as essentially a separate nation, and felt that the job of the black writer was to create the values by which his race would live and die.[16] However, he argued that ultimately a nationalist perspective did not go far enough, and that having broadened his consciousness through an understanding of the nationalistic folklore of his people, the black writer must transcend nationalism and transform his own personality through the Marxian conception of reality.

Now Harold Cruse in *The Crisis of the Negro Intellectual* has ably pointed out that the American imported and unadapted Marxism was a dead-end street, since it had no conception of the black reality nor any real intention of acquiring one.[17] As I have indicated, Wright was not unaware of the myopia of American Marxists. His positive gain was sufficient psychological distance from the American middle-class oriented cultural patterns to articulate perspectives and symbols of the black and white cultures. This gave him, at least, a version of the total American reality as it relates to Blacks. Although Wright had qualified his Marxist stance by stating that Marxism was the bare-bones upon which the black writer must graft the flesh, he did ask that the writer mould Negro folklore "with the concepts that move and direct the forces of history today," that is, with Marxism. The negative effects of this Marxism, as well as the emphatic convictions that derived from psychology and the social sciences, were that the very lights they provided for gaining power over certain aspects of black humanity, by their very glare, blinded him to others.

Take that fine group of short stories that comprise *Uncle Tom's Children*. On a first reading, the reader is overwhelmed by the sheer power of naturalistic form, out of which several stories explode upon him. In "Big Boy Leaves Home," Big Boy and his gang are discovered by a Southern white woman bathing in the nude in a Southern white man's creek. (The black man and the white woman are a Negro folklore theme.) Startled when they come toward her to get their clothes, she screams. Her nearby escort shoots and kills two of the boys, and Big Boy wrests the gun from him and kills him. With the help of the folk community and his family, Big Boy escapes, but his friend Bobo is brutally lynched by a mob. From his hiding place Big Boy witnesses the deed. He escapes the following morning in a truck bound for Chicago.

The story has been very justly admired. In the 1930's when the story first appeared the very type of lynching it described was horribly so much more than a mere literary reality. Black men, remembering the wariness with which they stepped around such women in real life and that lingering dread of being trapped with them in some unstructured situation where neither "racial etiquette" nor rational chat would absolve, could read and feel the stomach gone awry. Also that high, irreverence of boyhood smashed up against the System is so well pictured; the dialogue is so full of life, and the folk culture so carefully evoked—who could resist? Add to this powerful scenes, and narrative drive.

But then, a serious flaw. Wright's chief interest is in Big Boy—in his raw revolutionary will to survive and prevail. So that Wright forgets that youth does not experience the shooting down of two comrades and the horrible lynching of a third, without a sea change in its nature. But Big Boy remains simply pre-occupied with physical well-being, and casually explains how it went with his comrade, Bobo: "They burnt im. . . Will, ah wan some water; mah throats like fire."[18]

"Down By the Riverside" continues the emphasis upon the will to survive, although Mann, the main character, is killed by soldiers under emergency flood conditions. Mann is determined to get his pregnant wife to a doctor and his family to the hills away from flood waters that already swirl at his cabin door. In a stolen boat, he is forced to kill a white man. Mann pits his will against nature and whites. It is a brilliant but losing battle and he knows well before the events that he will be captured and killed.

He expresses will by determining the moment when he will die. In this way, he briefly affirms for the universe that Mann existed:

> Yes, now, he would die! He would die before he would let them kill him. Ah'll die fo they kill me! Ah'll *die*. . . . He ran straight to the right, through the trees, in the direction of the water. He heard a shot.[19]

Although he is killed by the soldiers, they have been forced to accept the time that he offers.

With "Long Black Song," the third story the focus is shifted. Silas, the character representing individual will, does not appear until the second half of the story. Wright instead focuses upon Silas's wife, a person conceived of as sunk-in-nature or as undifferentiated nature. The shift destroys the simply story line which Wright has followed. Blacks, uncommitted to struggle, in the earlier stories, were backstaged or absent.

Sarah, on the other hand, as a black person not emerged from nature, requires a creative energy to lift her from the category of stereotype which Wright was unable to give her. One has to see her as earth goddess or as the stereotype of loose sexuality. Since Silas's violent war with whites and his obvious needs and heroic struggle claim the sympathy of the reader, the symbols that have given Sarah a tenuous stature as earth goddess, above the wars of black and white men, crumble, and she appears as mere mindless stupidity and sensuality.

In her actions Sarah resists Western clock time. The sole clock in the house is out of repair. In an obviously symbolic action, her baby is unpacified when she holds him up to the sun (nature's time), but quietens when she allows him to beat upon the clock (Western time). She declares that they need no clock. "We just don't need no time, mistah."[20] Wright gears her responses to images of the season and its rhythms.

Dreaming secretly of Tom, a man with a similar emotional structure, Sarah is seduced by a white salesman, whose music and personality evoke her maternal feelings and a sense of harmonious nature. Silas, her husband, upon discovering betrayal kills the salesman and other white men. Again the choice factor of the stern willed: Facing a lynch mob, Silas insists upon determining the mode of his death by remaining in his burning house which the mob has set on fire.

Silas breaks out in one powerful nationalistic chant against the way the cards are stacked against him as a black man in the universe. He has accepted the world of time, materialistic struggle, and manipulation of Nature. He has worked for ten years to become the owner of his farm. Yet the tone and terms of his chant imply that the dread of the day of reckoning had long been on his mind: "He began to talk to no one in particular; he simply stood over the dead white man and talked out of his life, out of a deep and final sense that now it was all over and nothing could make any difference."

> "The white folks ain never gimme a chance! They ain never give no black man a chance! there ain nothin in your whole life yuh kin keep from 'em. They take yo lan. They take yo women! N' then they take yo life."[21]

In addition, he is stabbed in the back by "Mah own blood," i.e., his wife. At bottom, Silas is concerned about the meaning of his life.

This nationalistic base is also a part of the two preceding stories. In "Big Boy Leaves" home it is tacitly assumed. The folk elders" unspoken assumptions, the quickness with which they devise Big Boy's escape, and the white supremacy assumptions with which whites instantly and almost casually commit the most horrible violence, reflect nationalist stances. In "Down by the Riverside," a part of the same Nationalistic assumptions are operative, and Mann expresses a lament for the failure of himself and others to live up to the Nationalistic implications of their lives:

"For a split second he was there among those blunt and hazy black faces looking silently and fearfully at the white folks take some poor black man away. Why don they help me? Yet he knew they would not and could not help him, even as he in times past had not helped other black men being taken by the white folks to their death.[22]

In a vital creative formula, Wright has thus combined the idea of revolutionary will, embryonic nationalism, and Negro folklore moulded into a martial stance.

The pattern is continued in the last two stories, which differ from the first group by bringing the Communist movement into the picture and having the individual will relate to the group will. "Fire and Cloud" has the black minister Taylor to lead black and white workers in a march upon a Southern town, which has refused to relieve their hunger. At first Taylor's motivations are religious impulses and a concept of nature as communal. The tilling of the land brings organic satisfaction of great depth. But the whites have taken the land and confiscated nature. Taylor's will is strong. He endures vicious beatings by whites and learns that he must get with the people, if the problem is to be solved.

The last story "Bright and Morning Star" is superior to "Fire and Cloud," because it more carefully investigates the inner psychology of An Sue, a mother of communists, who gives up the image of Christ by which she has formerly shrunk from the world. Her nationalistic impulse is in her distrust for white comrades, a feeling which her son has enthusiastically transcended. An Sue, however, is all too prophetic. Booker, a poor white communist informer, tricks her into giving him the names of comrades, although her intuition sees him in the image of the oppressor, the "white mountain."

Now in order to see Johnny Boy, whom the mob has captured, and confirm her suspicions about Booker, she goes to the mob scene "lika nigga woman wid mah windin sheet t git mah dead son."[23] In the sheet she conceals a gun. Defiantly refusing to make her captured son inform, she endures his being maimed; then as Booker begins to inform, she kills him. She and her son are then killed by the mob, although "She gave up as much of her life as she could before they took it from her."[24]

The nationalist impulse thus overides both escapist religion and communism. She is between two worlds without the benefit of the "grace" that either might confer. The impulse that sustains her defiance is more than nationalist; it is that of revolutionary will, the demand for the right to give final shape to the meaning of one's life. In a word, like all the heroic characters of *Uncle Tom's Children,* her choice is existential. The device of the winding sheet, with which she asserts her will, will be recognized as a well known Negro folklore story.

As Wright's fictional scene moved to the urban ghetto, he encountered a new challenge because the forces that attacked the lives of black people were so often abstract and impersonal, unlike the Southern mob, sheriff or plantation owner. Yet out of the urban area was to come the most prophetic images relevant to the ordinary black man in the ghetto.

Although *Lawd Today* was first published in 1963, a statement in the bibliographical section of Constance Webb's *Richard Wright* notes that it "was probably written sometime between 1935 and 1937."[25] Constance Webb speaks of his working on a novel about post-office workers during the summer of 1935.[26] The book does have something of an exploratory air about it, and certainly does not immediately connect its wires to ideology or resound in defense of Blacks. I think that critics have been offended by the brutality and lower depth quality, which its black characters project. Wright's flaming defense of Blacks and indictment of whites had filled the vision of even mild-mannered black critics and given them the benefit of a genteel catharsis; therefore, it was very easy to miss the more negative attitudes that he held in regard to black life.

Yet, *Lawd Today* is very important in the study of Richard Wright for several reasons. It defines at least an essential part of black life, points up the importance of the inscriptions from other writings as aids to understanding his intentions, and enables us to see Wright examining a slice of black life practically on its own terms.

In addition to Wright's strictures on black life in *Black Boy*—cultural barrenness, lack of tenderness and genuine passion, etc., there had also appeared the statement that "I know that Negroes had never been allowed to catch the full spirit of Western Civilization, that they lived somehow in but not of it."[27] *Lawd Today* addresses itself to this situation. The title *Lawd Today,* a folk exclamation on confronting the events of the day, is to express a people who have not been able to make their life their own, who must live "from day to day." And as Conrad Kent Rivers put it in his poem on Wright—"To Live from Day to Day is not to live at all."

To compound the problem: Wright was perfectly capable of seeing emptiness as characteristic of the life of the ordinary white worker. In "The Man Who Went to Chicago,"[28] his white female co-workers in a restaurant exposed "their tawdry dreams, their simple hopes, their home lives, their fear of feeling anything deeply. . . ." Although they were casually kind and impersonal, "They knew nothing of hate and fear, and strove instinctively to avoid all passion." Their lives were totally given to striving "for petty goals, the trivial material prizes of American life." To become more than children, they would have to include in their personalities "a knowledge of lives such as I lived and suffered containedly." Wright is on his way to describing a shallowly optimistic America, one that avoided the tragic encounter and the knowledge to be derived therefrom, one that excluded blacks from "the entire tide and direction of American culture," although they are "an organic part of the nation. . . ."

A similarity, yes, and yet a difference. Wright seems to see ordinary white life by its intrinsic relationship to Western technology, as pulled into some semblance of order—one that is sufficient for superficial living, elementary assertion of will and materialistic acquisitiveness. On the other hand, Saunders Redding comments perceptively on one of Wright's objections to black life: Wright knew "that survival for the Negro depended upon his not making choices, upon his ability to adapt to choices (the will of others) made for him. He hated this. . . .[29] In his introduction to the 1945 edition of St Clair Drake and Horace R. Cayton's *Black Metropolis,* Wright more fully describes conditions which he feels deprives Modern Man of deep organic satisfaction, and programs the stunted and frenzied lives of Blacks.

As an expression of this extreme frustration, *Lawd Today* deserves a separate and more careful analysis than I can here give to it. Its universe provides its chief character, Jake Jackson, a Mississippi migrant, and his friends no true self-consciousness. It is a universe of violence, magic, quack medicine, numbers playing and dreambooks, roots and herbs, cheap movies, tuberculosis and venereal disease, hard liquor and sex and corrupt politics. The relation between Jake Jackson and his wife Lil is that of warfare; the book begins with Jake's brutal beating of her, and it ends with Jake's drunken attempt to beat her again, an event that sees her, in self-defense, knocking him unconscious.

> "Lawd, I wish I was dead," she [Lil] sobbed softly.
> Outside an icy wind swept around the corner of the building, whining and moaning like an idiot in a deep black pit.[30]

The brutal relations of Jake and Lil provide the one-day frame for the book. The only real value represented is the rough and ready fellowship between Jake and his friends—Al, whose pride stems from his membership in a national guard unit that breaks up strikes and leftist gatherings; Bob, who suffers throughout the story from a bad case of gonnorhea; and Slim, whose body is wracked with tuberculosis. Jake knows that something is missing from his life, but he can't pin it down. So he and his comrades turn to whatever will jolt their bodies into a brief illusion of triumphant living.

Wright uses several external devices in order to make his intentions apparent. For rather heavy-handed irony, he has the events to take place on Lincoln's birthday. The radio delivers a steady barrage of talk about the war that freed the slaves while Jake and his friends, spiritually lost and enslaved in urban society, fumble through the events of the day. Part I bears the inscription taken from Van Wyck Brooks's *America's Coming of Age* ". . . a vast Sargasso Sea —a prodigious welter of unconscious life, swept by groundwells of half-conscious emotion . . ." The inscription is obviously well-chosen, and is to be applied to the lives of Jake and his friends. Part II is entitled "Squirrel Cage," a section in which the characters' actions are no more fruitful that that of caged animals. An inscription from Waldo Frank's *Our America* speaks of the lives of men and women as "some form of life that has hardened but not grown and over which the world has passed. . . ." Part III takes both its title, "Rat's Alley," and its inscription from T. S. Eliot's *Wasteland:* ". . . But at my back in a cold blast I hear/The rattle of the bones, and chuckle spread from ear to ear." Thus the title headings and the inscriptions alert the reader to the themes of artificially stunted and sterile lives, half-conscious and inarticulate, and force a wider reference to their universe. Something very big and nasty is indeed biting the characters in *Lawd Today*, but it is part of the theme of the book that, though one character prays and most of the others beg, borrow, and "ball," they cannot name the water that would relieve their wasteland.

In concentrating upon simply presenting the lives and their surroundings, Wright displays gifts that are not the trademarks of his other novels. Sensational incidents do not threaten the principle of proportion, or make melodrama an end in itself. Of all things, Wright displays, in his opening portrait of Jake Jackson, a talent for biting satire! Humor, so limited in other works, is often wildly raucous. The gift for portraying extended scenes, apparent in other works and so important to the novelist, is still marvelously in evidence. So also is Wright's great talent for the recording of speech rhythms and color. In the character Al's narrative of a masochistic black woman, Wright even does credit to the tall story tradition.[81]

But his most astonishing performance is Section IV of "Squirrel Cage," in which, for thirty pages, all speeches are anonymous and the postal workers render communially their inner life and feelings.

> They had worked in this manner for so many years that they took one another for granted; their common feelings were common knowledge. And when they talked it was more like thinking aloud than speaking for purposes of communication. Clusters of emotion, dim accretions of instinct and tradition rose to the surface of their consciousness like dead bodies floating and swollen upon a night sea.[32]

Despite the negative simile about dead bodies, the speeches form a poem, a device which breaks the novel's tight realism and gives its rendering power a new dimension. It is strange that Wright did not develop the technique further, since his naturalism, in order to fully encompass his reach, required the supplement of his own intrusive commentary.

Lawd Today enlarges our perspective on *Native Son*, for it creates the universe of Bigger Thomas in terms more dense than the carefully chosen symbolic reference points of *Native Son*. The continuity of Wright's concerns stand out with great clarity and depth. Running through all Wright's works and thoroughly pervading his personality are his identification with and rejection of the

West, and his identification with and rejection of the conditions of black life. *Lawd Today* is primarily concerned with the latter.

In *Native Son, Wright's* greatest work, he returned to the rebel outsider, the character with revolutionary will and the grit to make existential choices. Bigger Thomas, like the heroic characters of *Uncle Tom's Children* finally insists upon defining the meaning of his life: ". . . What I killed for, I am," cries Bigger at the end of his violent and bloody life.

Wright early establishes the myth of the heritage of Man, Western Man, as a counterpoint to the disinherited condition of Bigger Thomas, a Southern black migrant with an eighth grade education. In the first section of the novel, Bigger expresses his frustration by violent and cowardly reactions, and by references to the rituals of power and freedom that he envies. What does he wish to happen, since he complains the nothing happens in his universe? "Anything, Bigger said with a wide sweep of his dingy palm, a sweep that included all the possible activities of the world."

> Then their eyes [Bigger's and his gang's] were riveted; a slate colored pigeon swooped down to the middle of the steel car tracks and began strutting to and from with ruffled feathers, its fat neck bobbing with regal pride. A street car rumbled forward and the pigeon rose swiftly through the air on wings stretched so taut and sheer that Bigger could see the god of the sun through their translucent tips. He tilted his head and watched the slate-colored bird flap and wheel out of sight over the ridge of a high roof.
>
> "Now, if I could only do that," Bigger said.[30]

Bigger, himself, instinctively realizes that a job and night school will not fundamentally alter his relationship to the universe. To the white and wealthy Mrs. Dalton's query concerning night school, his mind silently makes a vague response: "Night school was all right, but he had other plans. Well, he didn't know just what they were right now, but he was working them out."[34] As to the job with the Daltons, it is but an extension of the System that holds him in contempt and stifles his being: the "relief" people will cut off his food and starve his family if he does not take it. Because of the resulting pressure from his family for physical comfort and survival, ". . . he felt that they had tricked him into a cheap surrender." The job and night school would have programmed his life into conformity with what Wright called the "pet nigger system,"[35] but would not have gained respect for his manhood.

Bigger Thomas and Richard Wright were after the system—not merely its pieces.

A major source of the power of *Native Son* derived from Wright's ability to articulate the relevant rituals of black and white cultures—and Bigger's response to them. These rituals emphasize the presence in culture of rational drive, curiosity, revolutionary will, individualism, self-consciousness (preoccupations of Western culture)—or their absence.

Thus blindness (shared by white and black cultures), softness, shrinking from life, escapism, otherworldliness, abjectness, and surrender, are the meaning of the black cultural rituals from which Bigger recoils, and the counters with which Blacks are allowed to purchase their meager allowance of shelter and bread. They contrast sharply with Bigger's (the outsider's) deep urges for freedom of gesture and spontaneous response to existence. Wright's indictment is that these negative qualities are systematically programmed into black culture by the all powerful white oppressor.

Having murdered the white girl Mary Dalton—thus defying the imprisoning white oppressor, Bigger Thomas feels a rush of energy that makes him equal to the oppressor. He now explains his revolt against black culture. Buddy, his brother, is "soft and vague; his eyes were defenseless and their glance went only to the surface of things." Buddy is "aimless, lost, with no sharp or hard edges, like a chubby puppy." There is in him "a certain stillness, an isolation, meaninglessness."[36]

Bigger's sister Vera, "seemed to be shrinking from life with every gesture she made." His mother has religion in place of whiskey, and his girlfriend Bessie has whiskey in place of religion. In the last section of *Native Son,* his mother's epiphany is her crawling on her knees from one white Dalton to the other to beg for the life of Bigger. In "Flight," the second part of the novel, Bessie's epiphany is a prose blues complaint concerning the trap of her life, and then in a terrible sigh that surrenders to Bigger her entire will, she betrays her life completely. Finally, after Bigger is captured, a black minister epiphanizes the version of religious passivity that insured endurance of aimless and cramped life, as he unsuccessfully appeals to the captured Bigger. The gestures and rituals of the black minister are rendered with masterly brilliance.

In contrast, the symbols, rituals, and personalities of the white culture express directness, spontaneous freedom, at-homeness in the universe, will—and tyranny. While Bigger concentrates upon avoiding answering questions from the communist Jan Erlone and the liberal Mary Dalton in yes or no terms, he is confounded by their ability to act and speak simply and directly. In a very fine scene that evidences Wright's great novelistic talent, their very freedom and liberality dramatize his oppression and shame. Their gestures say that it is their universe. And the fact that Jan Erlone and Mary Dalton, in seconds, can, as individuals, suspend all racial restraints underlines the habitual racial rigidities ingrained in Bigger's life, which deprives him of spontaneous gesture. Oppressively, "To Bigger and his kind, white people were not really people; they were a sort of great natural force, like a stormy sky looming overhead, or like a deep swirling river stretching suddenly at one's feet in the dark." The white world is the "white blur," "white walls," "the snow,"—all of which place Bigger in the condition of the desperate rat with which *Native Son* begins.

The Jan Erlone—Dalton group of whites express the rituals mediated by a sufficient humanism to partially obscure their relationship to a brutal system. They inspire Bigger's hatred but also a measure of bewilderment. Even the elder Dalton can be nice because the System does the work. With one hand he functions in a company that restricts Blacks to ghettos and squeezes from them high rents for rat infested, cramped apartments; with the other, and without conscious irony, he gives substantial sums to black uplift organizations. Although the Dalton's kindness cannot extend to sparing Bigger's life (since he has murdered their daughter—the flower of the system), he will prevent the ejection of Bigger's family from its rat dominated apartment.

The liberalism of the Communist Jan Erlone, his girl friend sympathizer Mary Dalton, and the rest of the Dalton family function as esthetic rituals that create an easy-going atmosphere for sullen submission and inhibition. In the militarized zone are the racial rituals of Detective Britten bouncing Bigger's head against the wall and spitting out definitions of Blacks that deny their life.

Then there are the agents of the mass media, the rhetoricians, the police, and the mob.

Bigger standing equally outside the shrinking black culture and the hard-driving white culture can only feel the existential choice demanded by his compulsion toward the heritage of man shoving upward from his guts, and sense that something very terrible must happen to him. Near the end he is tortured by the knowledge that his deepest hunger is for human communion, and by his lawyer's briefly raising it as a possibility. But the mirage is soon exposed and he must warm himself by the bleak embers of his hard-won and lonely existential knowledge: ". . . what I killed for, I am!"

It is part of the greatness of *Native Son* that it survives a plethora of flaws. For example, despite Wright's indictment of white society, he shows in his major fiction little knowledge that, while black life is stifled by brutality, the private realities of white life find it increasingly impossible to free themselves from the imprisoning blandishments of a neurotic culture. His failure to image this fact, although we have seen that he had some understanding of it, makes it seem that Bigger's problems would have been solved by his entry into the white world. The great engagement of the universe that rages through the first and second parts of the novel sputters, at points, in the third part while Wright scores debater's points on jobs, housing, and equal opportunity. The famous courtroom speech that the attorney Max makes in behalf of Bigger hardly rises above such humanitarian matters. Thus a novel that resounds in revolutionary tones descends to merely reformist modulations that would make glad the heart of a New Deal liberal.

As the theme and situations of the novel increase in density of implication, Wright is too frequently touching the reader's elbow to explain reactions and make distinctions that are too complex for Bigger to verbalize. The style, therefore, fails at crucial points. Melodrama, as in the murder of Mary Dalton, is sometimes very functional. At other times, it is unfortunately its own excuse for being.

And so one may go on, but when he finishes he will find *Native Son* still afloat and waiting for the next reader to make it a reference point in the fabric of his being.

Wright's vision of black men and women rendered in the four books that I have discussed stormed its way into the fabric of

American culture with such fury that its threads form a reference point in the thinking and imagination of those who have yet to read him. Quickly downgraded as more art-conscious black writers made the scene, he seems now all too prophetic, and all too relevant, majestically waiting that close critical engagement which forms the greatest respect that can be paid to a great man and writer.

Thus, today, when we think that we know so much about black life, even down to its metaphysics and ambiguity, it is humbling to realize that the lifelong commitment of soul that was Richard Wright is of the essence of much that we think we know.

FOOTNOTES

1. W. E. B. DuBois, *The Souls of Black Folk* (New York: Fawcett Publications, 1963), p. 18.
2. Frantz Fanon, *Black Skin, White Masks* (New York, 1967), p. 116.
3. See Ralph Ellison, *Shadow and Act* (New York, 1964), pp. 134-135; Constance Webb, *Richard Wright* (New York, 1968) p. 205. See also notes to this Chapter (XIV). From Miss Webb's discussion of *Black Boy*, I deduce that he was still too close psychologically to his youth to give a rounded picture.
4. Richard Wright, *Black Boy* (New York, 1945), p. 52.
5. Webb, p. 205.
6. *Black Boy*, p. 73.
7. *Ibid.*, p. 190.
8. Webb, p. 186. Hollywood had asked Wright to write a screen play of *Up From Slavery*.
9. DuBois, pp. 16-18.
10. Ralph Ellison, "Recent Negro Fiction," *New Masses* (August 5, 1941), p. 25.
11. *Shadow and Act.* pp. 119-120.
12. Richard Wright, *Eight Men* (New York, 1961), pp. 161-191.
13. Richard Crossman, ed., *The God that Failed* (New York: Bantam, 1952), pp. 103-146.
14. Crossman, p. 108.
15. Webb, pp. 320-322.
16. Richard Wright, "Blueprint for Negro Writing," *New Challenge* (Fall, 1937), pp. 53-64.
17. Harold Cruse, *The Crisis of the Negro Intellectual* (New York, 1967), pp. 181-189. See also his *Rebellion of Revolution* (New York, 1968),
18,
19, *Ibid,,* p, 93,
20. *Ibid.*, p.98.
21. *Ibid.*, p. 113.
22. *Ibid.*, p. 88.
23. *Ibid.*, p. 185.
24. *Ibid.*, p. 192.

25. Webb, p. 424.
26. Webb, p. 135.
27. *Black Boy*, p. 33.
28. *Eight Men*, pp. 168-170.
29. Herbert Hill, *Anger and Beyond* (New York, 1966), p. 209.
30. Richard Wright, *Lawd Today* (New York, 1963), p. 224.
31. *Ibid.*, pp. 158-161. See also an apparent reworking of the story in Eldridge Cleaver, *Soul on Ice* (New York, 1968), pp. 166-169.
32. *Lawd Today*, p. 162.
33. Richard Wright, *Native Son* (New York: Signet, 1961), pp. 23-24.
34. *Ibid.*, p. 62.
35. Webb, p. 205.
36. *Native Son*, p. 103.

On the
Future Study
of Richard Wright

IN THE 1950'S LITERARY OPINION MAKERS WERE IN A great hurry to clear the stage of Richard Wright and to make room for more art-conscious black writers. Critical generalizations and intuitive judgments hardened into critical party lines, and since the stormy sociological surface of Wright's works was the focus of the liberal establishment, there was a tendency to insist that the issues which he raised were completely topical—issues, it was thought, that were being speedily resolved by liberal emotions, New Deal legislation, Supreme Court edicts, NAACP persistence, and Freedom Marches. And suddenly, the halo of the integration struggle sizzled with third-degree burns in the flames of a hundred cities. If those bewildered and snarling black faces that rose up from television screens to haunt our minds and souls were not the exact replicas of Bigger Thomas, his family, and friends, they sure sounded like real close kin.

Thus Richard Wright now seems real relevant. Once criticized for committing himself to deprived and inarticulate heroes whose sensibilities could not possibly grasp the big picture, Wright now appears to have anticipated the urban upheavals, the alienation and the violence of our times (an achievement which was beyond the capacity of sociologists). Indeed, he is yet the lone black writer to look so carefully into the psychology of the ordinary mass of black minds, and to understand that when their stake in the dignity of

Reprinted from *CLA Journal, XII,* No. 4, June, 1969.

Man was no longer legally programmed out of existence, a soulless technology would have sufficient rhythm to complete the job with no loss of momentum.

So much for contemporary relevance.

It is important for leading us to the discovery that insufficiently recognized themes emerge from the vital depths of Wright's works: the growth of consciousness and reclaiming the heritage of man.

It is important for impelling us to render the tribute due a writer of Wright's great creative talent: close critical engagement and thorough absorption.

So impelled, we ask what is to be done in the study of Wright? The answer that comes back to us is, "Everything."

II

I shall not attempt to outline everything, however, but to suggest approaches which, when completed, will suggest additional needs. First, the work that will make other studies more informed and solid.

A. *Biography and Bibliography.* Although Constance Webb's *Richard Wright* provides needed information, a more comprehensive biography that emerges from an independent but sympathetic perspective is desperately required. More specialized biographies, as well as more informed criticism, could then develop. This area has special urgency, since the job has to be done while many people with personal knowledge of Wright are still alive. As to bibliography, this seems to be developing at a good pace. Constance Webb's reprint of the Fabre-Margolies bibliography in her *Richard Wright,* and its further reprint in the January (1969) Issue of *Negro Digest* make a good listing easily available. However, there is room for additions and for various types of bibliography.

B. *Collected Works and Other Collections.* There is neither an established set of texts nor a sufficient number of hardback titles in print. The Wright student is thus at the mercy of paperbacks that are subject to casual editing for popular commercial consumption. A definitive standard edition is desirable and would probably pay for itself at this time of high interest in Black Studies. At the least, some editing must begin while manuscript versions of Wright's works are in the hands of sympathetic persons.

Other types of collections are needed for other purposes. A single well-edited book should bring all autobiographical material together. A Wright portable or reader is needed to reveal Wright in cross-section and at his best. A collection of significant criticism of Wright would make available a few gems that are now gathering dust on library shelves, and serve to suggest new directions for the critic.

C. *Full-Length Studies.* Here I shall simply suggest a few types that seem to be mandatory and groundbreaking. A simple survey type of study that covered Wright extensively and stated issues broadly would define areas that others could follow up. Biographical memoirs that helped to suggest relationships between the man and his work, especially of the type which Ralph Ellison could produce, would retain a humanizing influence upon more abstract types of studies. Perhaps numerous critical analyses are needed. Despite the naturalistic simplicity that Wright's works seem to promise, the careful reader will find that Wright calculated nicely. He was a very conscious writer, a craftsman and an experimentalist, who familiarized himself with the variety of devices afforded by modernist fiction. Thus the glib pronouncement once circulated that a Wright book takes everything seriously but the writing, is the first deadend street that the wary critic would do well to avoid.

Although too many brief studies have been sociological, it does not follow that a thoroughgoing, full-length sociological study is not needed. Wright's personal background, his fascination with the social sciences as tools for analyzing society and personality, his varied use of sociology, would seem to demand such a study. There is also the fact that certain sociological and anthropological concepts seem now to have been ill-digested, and here the esthetic cannot completely be separated from the sociological. Further, a study of his mind and art will have to bear a strain of sociological inquiry. A sufficient tendency toward the study of his art in its own terms now prevails, and will serve as corrective of false emphases.

Closely allied with sociological study, would be a systematic and evaluative study of Wright's reading. Inscriptions that form part of the meaning of a Wright book, the dependence that he placed upon reading in shaping his concept, his interest in Marx and other social philosophers, and his seizure of psychological theory, suggest the crucial importance of his reading. Then there is the probability of significant gaps, and sometimes, too great an openness to theories. It is sobering, for example, to learn from Constance Webb's *Richard Wright* that as late as 1940, when Wright was thirty-two, he had not read Booker T. Washington's *Up From Slavery*. It is also possible that, at that time, he did not have an intimate knowledge of major figures in black history—a fact which may have had something to do with his feeling, as expressed in *Black Boy*, that black life lacked the tender and heroic qualities. Then there is the impact of specific works. O. Mannoni's *Prospero and Caliban, The Psychology of Colonialism*, for example, a work which argues that a dependency complex and an unconscious wish for domination by the invader existed in the minds of colonized people before the arrival of the colonizer. Wright read Mannoni, according to Constance Webb, prior to his trip to Africa. Without being able to state cause and effect, or influence, we can only repeat Wright's words: that he found the African a very oblique and hard-to-know man.

The final suggestion for a book-length, groundbreaking type of study is that an analysis be made of Wright's relations with the Communist Party.

D. *The Briefer Essay or Monograph.* The approach here can be defined by two questions. What generalizations (and cliche judgments) require close examination? What, in general, is missing most in approaches that have already been made?

First the category of generalizations and cliche judgments, which sometimes give the illusion of bearing the stamp of divine authority. Wright, for example, is under the blanket indictment of offering unmotivated violence. An informed judgment on Wright's use of violence would study carefully its psychological source and forms and indicate the relative degree of motivation or non-motivation apparent in specific works. In other words, one has to come by Wright's preoccupation with bottled-up emotions that imply unconventional time-schedules for explosion. Then there is the question of melodrama; the logical literary question is not whether it is present but whether it is *functional*. Other subjects that exemplify the category: effectiveness of style in relationship to intention; limitations in development of character; conflict between propaganda and art; the significance of naturalistic form and complexity of subject; the reconciling of nationalist subject matter with integrationist aims; relationship between Wright and his audience; and other subjects such as these suggest.

Then—what seems to be, in general, conspicuous by absence or scarcity in existing brief studies? No one has made a commanding appraisal of Wright's influence upon other black writers. Therefore, the field is left to the negative reservations of James Baldwin and Ralph Ellison, who rightfully feel that they should not be confined within Wright's shadow. Still, it is obvious that Baldwin has not outgrown completely the early influence of Wright. And there are striking parallels in situations, argumentation, and judgments, that would emerge in a comparative study of Wright's *Black Boy* and Ellison's *Invisible Man.* A balanced study should do justice to the impact of Wright and the areas of uniqueness among other black writers.

Wright's work also invites the kind of psychological study that throws light upon it and himself. His relationship to his mother, for example, was highly tensioned, although devoted, a fact which may have influenced the rather constricted roles permitted to women characters in his fiction. A suggestive corollary is the limited relationships that exist between his men and women characters. Imagery, repetitive themes and tensioned situations, the roots of racial conflict, the use of dreams and other devices—all these will yield to a disciplined psychological approach to further insight upon both the man and his work.

For all we know, the whole area of Wright's reactions to life outside the United States that influenced the creation of some of his fiction and the formation of non-fictional studies of Spain. African countries, and the East, may require a longer examination than an article or a monograph would afford. However, the groundwork could certainly consist of a series of brief and separate investigations. Wright's reactions abroad constitute an important phase of his development.

The suggestions for shorter essays and monographs, of course, can be endless. I end, therefore, with a listing of much needed analyses of an artistic kind: an updated study of the art of his short stories; separate revaluations of individual stories, novels, and autobiography; a study of *connections* between individual works

(*Native Son, Lawd Today,* and *The Long Dream,* for example); his use of folk sources; patterns of his poetry; natural and conscious tendencies toward the existential posture; his literary criticism; his use of dialect; and comparative studies of his published works with their manuscript versions.

Now—may the mills of graduate schools and those of others begin to grind surely, but not too slowly.

The Poetry
of
Gwendolyn Brooks

GWENDOLYN BROOKS SHARES WITH LANGSTON
Hughes the achievement of being most responsive to turbulent
changes in the black community's vision of itself and to the changing forms of its vibrations during decades of rapid change. The
depth of her responsiveness and her range of poetic resources make
her one of the most distinguished poets to appear in America during
the 20th Century.

She shares with Margaret Walker the achievement of summing
up the black mood of the 1940's: Margaret Walker in her famous
poem, "For My People"; and Gwendolyn Brooks in "Negro Hero,"
whose memorable image is that of a black ambivalent man laying
his life on the line for the sake of a "white gowned democracy"
with a dagger for his heart's blood up her sleeve. "Riders to the
Blood Red Wrath" (*Selected Poems,* 1963) more than any other
poem renders the black mood of the 1950's and early 1960's. It
dramatizes the inner attitudes, from which blacks expended great
spiritual resources under the leadership of Martin Luther King, Jr.

During the 1960's, the deepest poem to portray the deadened
hopelessness of urban Blacks which exploded in the city rebellions
was (and is) "In the Mecca" which appeared in a book by that title
in 1968. It portrays the misery, beauty, and frustration of black
occupants of a once existing huge apartment building in Chicago,
in which were jammed roughly 2,000 people. The book *In The
Mecca* also contains dramatic poems and portraits reflecting the

poet's absorption of the tensions implying revolutionary change and nationhood which arose during the late 1960's. Surrounding such peaks are simply poems which probe at great depth the daily dues-paying lives of "ordinary" people, who must act out the ultimates of their existence bereft of grand stages or the grand lines provided by a set script. Perhaps the publication of Miss Brooks's collected poetry (with the exception of the poignant children's poems *Bronzeville Boys and Girls*, 1956) in September, 1971, will place her poetic contributions in commanding perspective, and reveal that underneath the poet's restless changes and responses is an unchanging steel of commitment.

It was this unchanging steel of commitment which provided the basis for the mutual shock of recognition between Miss Brooks and the new young radical black poets. She was inspired by the raw, new, and bold expression of the young poets—by their seeming to be what Margaret Walker had called for in 1940: "Let a new race of men now rise and take control." They saw in her an inspiration, an example of brilliant writing, long-committed to the community, a foundation, a bridge. As evidenced by the wide range of reference to her poetry in *To Gwen With Love* (1971), which contains poems and other works in tribute to her influence and achievement, black poets of radical and other persuasions had experienced an impact from her that was wide and deep. As Hoyt Fuller points out in the forward to the tributes, the response was nationwide, and "it is fair to assume that none paid her homage merely on the basis of her great public fame" but either to the dedicated woman, mother, artist, community worker, known particularly to Chicagoans or to the person who had deeply touched them in one way or another. Variations of this touch had been experienced by the national community of black poets.

Thus Miss Brooks's current way with the expression of black tensions must be seen as a natural organic progression and growth. Although the poet gained an inspiration during the 60's which provided further extension of herself and her vision, and approach to community, the experience was not that sudden hot conversion on the road to Damascus so absolutely required by the inner weather of a St. Paul! Blacks who see in her writing a sudden "homecoming" are often celebrating a return trip of their own. White critics who bemoan the loss of the "pure poet of the human condition" reveal that they have not understood the depths of the body of her work, nor the source of her genuine universality. Despite the erratic approach of many white critics (one which really began with the publication of *The Bean Eaters,* 1960), Miss Brooks continues to receive the universal recognition which the quality of her poetry demands.

For the rest of this essay my concern will be with matters of form, sensibility, and the light upon the poet's achievement provided by poems selected from the body of her work. I begin with form.

But here I must be careful to identify Miss Brooks's way with form and technique and to avoid the common garden variety of connotations which they evoke. For example, she has pointed out repeatedly that she is neither form conscious nor an intellectual, and that she writes from the heart without making conscious decisions about form.[2] A partial exception to her usual practice was the decision which she made prior to writing the sonnet series concerning the dilemma of soldiers at war, "Gay Chaps at the Bar" (included in *A Street in Bronzeville* and *Selected Poems*). Before writing the first sonnet (with no thought of creating a series), she did decide that it would be written in "off-rhyme" because she felt that her subject, the consciousness of soldiers at war, was an "off-rhyme" situation.[3] That is, soldiers-at-war is not an experience that is necessarily to be celebrated by the full harmonic sound that conventional rhyme delivers, but by the edginess (sometimes, dis-harmony or dissonance) which deliberately chosen "imperfect" rhymes can render.

Thus, although in conventional rhyme the rhyming words have the same sounds in "their stressed vowels and all sounds following" but unlike sounds *preceding* the stressed vowels, Miss Brooks, in the opening sonnet of "Gay Chaps at the Bar," rhymes "dash" and "lush," with stressed vowels "u" and "a" unlike in sound. Deciding later to write a series of sonnets on the war situation, she created additional sonnets in conformity with the off-rhyme pattern.

> I said, there are other things to say about what's going on at the front [Second World War] and all, and I'll write more poems, some of them based on the stuff of letters that I was

getting from several soldiers, and I felt it would be good to have them all in the same form, because it would serve my purpose throughout.[4]

Miss Brooks's usual practice is to lean upon an intuitive sense of the form appropriate to her subject. Thus in an interview with George Stavros, Managing Editor of *Contemporary Review,* Miss Brooks could confess uncertainty as to why she used a modified form of the Chaucerian Rhyme Royal stanza for "The Anniad" (*Annie Allen*) but then suggest the intuitive basis for her choice: ". . . but I imagine I finished one stanza, then decided that the rest of them would be just like that."[5]

I should add here that by "intuitive sense" of appropriate form, I mean a discovery concerning form and fitness and *discoveries* (often not consciously articulated) concerning fit techniques made *during* the moment of creation. I mean a *feeling sense* of such matters—and *not* a Chairman of the Board type of decision.

It is well to stress the above principle on the basis of the "Anniad," since it is the most consciously developed poem among Miss Brooks's creations. She, herself, points out that it is a "labored poem," "a poem that's very interested in the mysteries and magic of technique." Though not trying to do something new, she "was just very conscious of every word; I wanted every phrase to be beautiful, and yet to contribute sanely to the whole, to the whole effect." The poem is thus closely and carefully textured in every stanza: ". . . every one [stanza] was worked on and revised, tenderly cared for, more than anything else I've written, and it is not a wild success; some of it just doesn't come off. But it was enjoyable."

The comments reveal Miss Brooks's love for the creative moment: "What a pleasure it was to write that poem!" But also revealed are the roles of revision and devoted work. She acknowledges that conscious shaping of form and selections among techniques occur during the process of revision. "The Anniad," though an extreme case, thus highlights approaches that are, in different degrees, intrinsic to the total body of her published poetry. Her comments finally reflect a stern self-criticism and, above all, a reverence for the magic inherent in words to which the poet must do justice.

It should also be noted Miss Brooks's intuition is one educated by years of workshop struggle and by saturation in progressive 20th Century poetry and aspects of the 19th Century. In an interview with Ida Lewis, former editor of *Essence,* she speaks of her early exposure to Paul Laurence Dunbar, a family idol, and important communication with James Weldon Johnson and Langston Hughes.[6] Through Countee Cullen's *Caroling Dusk,* an anthology of black poetry, she became acquainted with black writers of whom she had not heard before. One reading experience helped to define an approach to life which has become a hallmark of her work: "I read Langston Hughes's *Weary Blues,* for example and got very excited about what he was doing. I realized that writing about the ordinary aspects of black life was important.[7] (Earlier, her subjects had been nature, love, death, flowers, and the sky, with a fascinated fixation upon the beauty of clouds.) As everybody who has had casual contact with Gwendolyn Brooks's poetry knows, the devotion to "the ordinary aspects of black life" is the hallmark of her poetry.

Her intuition is educated by contact with a variety of poets and simply writers. In Herbert Hill's *Soon One Morning,* she listed as her "admirations" Chekhov, Emily Dickinson, John Crowe Ransom, Langston Hughes, and the Joyce of a group of short stories, *The Dubliners.*[8] She also acknowledges the T. S. Eliot of such poems as "Portrait of a Lady," "The Love Song of Alfred Prufrock," "The Hollow Men," and "The Wasteland"; and Merrill Moore, a member of a Southern based group of poets called The Fugitives, who composed thousands of sonnets in colloquial and conversational idiom devoted largely to the "ordinary" aspects of life. Miss Brooks has a respect, though not a liking, for Ezra Pound as a master of language. Others could probably be mentioned, since she is very widely read.

In her first volume of poetry *A Street in Bronzeville,* a favorite of Blacks, Miss Brooks reflects, it seems to me, the predominant influence of Langston Hughes and other black writers, although the influence of other modernist poets is evident. I would suggest that Hughes's influence is apparent in such poems as "When Mrs. Martin's Booker T.," "A Song in the Front Yard," "Patent Leather," the series of "Hattie Scott" poems, and "Queen of the Blues," although Miss Brooks frequently manages a distance of perspective and a gentle satire and humor which have their source in her own sensibility and values. This distance also derives from wide knowledge of such modernist techniques as irony; unusual conjunctions of words to evoke a complex sense of reality (Satin Legs Smith rising "in a clear delirum"); squeezing the utmost from an image ("The Negro Hero"—democracy as his "fair lady, with her knife lying cold, straight, in the softness of her sweet-flowing sleeve"); agility with mind-bending figurative language, sensitivity to the music of the phrase, instead of imprisonment in traditional line beats and meter; experimentation with the possibilities of *free verse* and various devices for sudden emphasis and verbal surprise; and authoritative management of tone and a wide-ranging lyricism.

The education of Miss Brooks's formal intuition in the broad storehouse of modernist techniques and the implications of forms was suddenly widened in July, 1941, when Inez Stark Boulton, a wealthy woman committed to the arts, began a poetry workshop for Blacks at the South Side Community Art Center, Chicago, which continued for almost two years. Miss Brooks has stated that it was in the workshop that she learned "more about modern poetry—from one who had an excellent understanding of it," and also a good deal about technique.[9] The text was Robert Hillyer's *First Principles of Verse*. The Pulitzer Prize winning traditionalist poet gives emphasis to the importance of traditional technique, and thus supplements the workshop's exposure to principles of modern poetry. Miss Brooks no longer feels, however, that *First Principles* is a good text for the young or beginning poet.[10]

Miss Brooks revealed in her first book considerable technical resources, a manipulation of folk forms, a growing sense of how traditional forms must be dealt with if the power of the black voice is to come through with integrity. *A Street in Bronzeville* (1945) committed its author to a restless experimentation with an elaborate range of artistic approaches. Although there are particular peaks in Miss Brooks's experimental approaches, such as those commonly recognized in *Annie Allen* (1949), her experimental ways have continued throughout her career. Since the late 1960's she has been committed to the creation of a simplicity from which the man who pauses reflectively at his glass in the tavern may gain a sense of the depth and meaning of black lives. To get the specific feeling of this simplicity, in comparison with an earlier poem whose message is similar, one might turn from a reading of Sonnet 2 of "The Children of the Poor" *(Annie Allen) to* "Women in Love-II" *(Family Pictures,* 1970). The comparison will reveal that the second poem achieves its simplicity by the stark directness of its trajectory, not by an evasion of the complexity of experience, whereas, the first carries a considerable load of explanation and carefully projected nuance as sources of complexity and depth. Each poem, of course, is a fine example of its type. The second poem, addressed primarily to a black audience, can assume that the audience will supply many of the nuances that in the first poem had to be either explicitly stated or skillfully suggested.

But a final comment on what I have called Miss Brooks's educated intuitional approach to discovery of appropriate form. I have stated that usually her way involves a discovery of appropriate form while in the process of composition, and further shaping in the revision process.

It seems to me that her method of composition provided her with certain rewards and protections as she moved among forms heavy with the vibrations of tradition. An intimate knowledge of traditional forms, for example, can provide an understanding also of their limitations, and thus offer the artist encouragement, assurance, and a further defined ground for experimentation. Such possibilities would certainly offer themselves to a poet with a "feeling sense" for form. A form which invites experimentation is the ballad, since it is essentially at the furtherest distance from the literary forms of very artificial traditions. In the many variations that Miss Brooks plays upon ballad form, she takes advantage of its flexibility, as can be seen by comparing such pieces as "Sadie and Maud," "The Ballad of Chocolate Mabbie," and "Southeast Corner" (A Street in Bronzeville). Also "of De Witt Williams on his way to Lincoln Cemetery" or (in The Bean Eaters) "The Ballad of Rudolph Reed." Miss Brooks's freedom with the ballad form may here be described in general terms: movement in different poems between the poles of the literary and traditional folk ballads, with some forays into the aspects of the black folk ballad; ("Queen of the Blues," A Street in Bronzeville); a deliberate evoking of the tone of the 16th Century ballad, by means of one of its standard rhythms and the use of some of its set phrases; a movement of the form closer to the immediacy of contemporary life, by means of devices for subtle nuances and varied pacing.

Another form which does not necessarily impose the connotations and nuances of a set tradition upon the black writer is *free verse,* since it is without either a set number of beats to the line or a requirement to rhyme. Mainly, the signature which Walt Whitman stamped upon its use served to place it in the public domain for further modifications by subsequent writers. Miss Brooks, it must suffice to say here, has over a long period developed a highly economical free verse line, varying in length to suit the music of the phrase and voice tones, and accommodating itself to rhymes placed here and there for special emphasis.

It will be seen that one can get a wide sampling of Miss Brooks's command over a well disciplined free verse through the long poem "In the Mecca" and her latest book, *Family Pictures.*

The obvious flexibility of such forms as the ballad and free verse suggests that where forms are not saturated with commanding connotations from Euro-American tradition the black writer can make easy-going alliances with them. But there are others which are more selfconsciously literary and so evocative of European tradition that they threaten to cancel out a sense of the immediacy of the black experience. All artists portraying unconventional experience face the threat to a degree, but for a black writer it assumes a peculiar degree of intensity. The problem is further intensified by writers who place such an indelible signature upon a particular form that it seems completely exhausted by them. The sonnet (which Miss Brooks frequently used) is an obvious example. And critics have both marveled and coughed nervously in confronting Phyllis Wheately's use of the heroic couplet in conformity with the style of Alexander Pope: an 18th Century representative of (and therefore bearing its connotation) a highly ordered and sophisticated upper class society.

The outcome of such uses can be that the black writer, while making interesting comments about the black experience, seems to be taking care of somebody else's business. Thus Countee Cullen, in trying for the sensuous style of John Keats—the 19th Century Romantic, seems, at times, to be taking care of Keats's business. Claude McKay, more often than it is comfortable to experience, seems, in part, to be taking care of the business of Byron and Shelley.

It is, I think, Miss Brooks's intuitional approach to form which usually enables her to render the illusion of taking care of nobody's business but her own, although one can hear muted echoes of other poets. The situation may be here briefly illustrated through her use

111

of the sonnet—a form bearing the commanding signatures of such masters as Shakespeare, Milton, and William Wordsworth. In reading her sonnets, one may notice that, possibly with an assist from the example of the already mentioned Merrill More, she won a freedom from its traditional rigidity and formal eloquence. She attacked the sonnet's rigidity by breaking up traditional sentence syntax into punctuated phrases, by emphasizing the colloquial, and by the pressure of her contemporary realism. In winning a freedom from traditional formal eloquence, however, she won also a freedom to use at will her own style of formal eloquence without being constricted by tradition. As a matter of fact, some of her best sonnets are in a formal eloquence and a somewhat traditional syntax, as evidenced by sonnet 2 of "The Children of the Poor."

The result of Miss Brooks's way with form and technique is usually a legitimate universalism. That is her poems tend not to represent a reach for some pre-existing Western universal to be arrived at by reducing the tensions inherent in the black experience. Their universalism derives, instead, from complete projection of a situation or experience's *space* and *vibrations* (going down deep, not transcending). Even where a pre-existing universal may be paraphrasable, the true roots of the poet's universalism are in her power of enforcing the illusion that the vibrations from the space her imagination has encircled are captured and focused with all the power and significance which the raw materials afforded. As evidence for the foregoing judgments, one could cite at random such short poems as "Kitchenette Apartment," "Southeast Corner," selected sonnets from *A Street in Bronzeville;* "Do Not be Afraid of No," selected sonnets from "The Womanhood" series and "Clogged and Soft and Sloppy Eyes" *(Annie Allen);* "Big Bessie Throws Her Son Into the Street," *(Selected Poems);* "Medgar Evers," *(In the Mecca);* and "To Don at Salaam" *(Family Pictures).* Among the longer poems, one thinks immediately of portions of *The Anniad,* "Riders to the Blood Red Wrath," and "In the Mecca."

What I have suggested so far argues for and points to a tough and finely tuned sensibility (characteristic emotional, psychic, and intellectual response to existence).

On the basis of Miss Brooks's well known devotion for her fellowman and the values informing her poetry, I would say that one source of her sensibility is a religious consciousness, from which dogma has been ground away. What remains is a muscular religious reflex, guided, to paraphrase a line from one of her poems, by eyes which retain the light that bites and terrifies.

On the basis of Miss Brooks's testimony concerning the qualities of the lives of her parents,[11] it is possible to assume that her reflex has its roots in what her father and mother offered from the deepest level of traditional black religious response—not the level which Blacks unacquainted with the depth of their folk tradition understand within the flat categories of "narcotic" or "escapism." And not the simple category of Jesus as the white folks' eternal superstar—an instrument for consoling whites and making right their strange and bloody deeds while calling Blacks and other breeds without the law only apparently to "God," but really to the ways, service, and brainwashing machine of white men.

No.

But black religious response on the still deeper level described by Paul Radin, the anthropologist, in his "Foreword" to *God Struck Me Dead,* a collection of post-Civil War conversion experiences edited by Clifton H. Johnson.[12] Basing his judgment upon a close study of black religious testimonials, Radin saw the great depths of black religious experience as a turning away from *disintegration,* an achievement of a status which the black, himself, has ordained from within, a striving for some form of harmony, and a rebirth as cosmic man. Accordingly, Radin points out, "Any ordered framework would have done. That of Christianity happened to be at hand." In Radin's version, the pre-Civil War Black was not converted to God, but converted God to himself. This was done because he "needed a fixed point, for both within and outside of himself he could see only vacillation and endless shifting." The result of the religious experience, at such a depth, was a "unified personality" which, because of the hard realism of a people set upon and crowded by outrageous life, did not become *mystic* but committed itself to life.

Perhaps we may quarrel with Radin's idea that any "ordered framework would have done," and modify the statement to read, "Any ordered framework which could deal with the root uncertainity (Radin's "vacillation and endless shifting") at the base of the center of being." As Prof. Charles Long, of the Divinity School, University of Chicago, points out, the probability is that Blacks were attracted to the Old Testament, not simply because the Hebrews were enslaved like themselves, but because stories of the Old Testament powerfully acknowledge the root uncertainties of existence (What philosophers call radical contingency) which they, themselves, were experiencing.[13]

The upshot of all this is that as late as the World War I period, which encompassed Miss Brooks's birth and her subsequent early childhood, people of the stripe of her parents, David and Keziah Brooks, had available a religion which enabled them to make simple but heroic decisions concerning the ordering of life and the commanding of whatever social space they could occupy. Thus, despite the fact that Mr. Brooks, who had aspired to become a doctor and had taken the first year of a premedical course at Fisk, was crowded into a corner by poverty and spent his life as a janitor, he could make the decision to create a kind and ordered life for his children, and could contribute to their cultural development. In the poem "In Honor of David Anderson Brooks, My Father," Miss Brooks was able to speak of him as "He who was Goodness, Gentleness, and Dignity . . ."

As to her mother who had been an elementary school teacher in Kansas, one gets from Miss Brooks's remarks that she is a person of will, duty, and religious certainity. As in the case of Claude McKay, Miss Brooks's talent for poetry was a home discovery; McKay's by his brother; Miss Brooks's by her mother who persuaded Gwendolyn to believe that her vocation was poetry and told her that she was to become the female Paul Laurence Dunbar. As to her mother's religion, Miss Brooks gives its depth and simplicity in a single sentence: "She feels firmly that you must pray, and that only good can come of it."[14]

In the interview with Ida Lewis Miss Brooks gives a very simple and direct picture of her own religious sensibility of the 1940's and 1950's: here she explains that she had believed that "All we had to do was keep on appealing to the whites to help us and they would. . . . Because I believed in Christianity. People were really good, I thought; there was some good even in people who seemed to be evil."[15] The evidence of the poetry, however, ranges from gentle questioning to skepticism. In her first volume, for example, the sonnet "God Works in a Mysterious Way" demands that God take care of the world's business, "Or we assume a sovereignty ourselves." In "The Anniad," the young black woman is she "Whom the higher gods forgot, Whom the lower gods berate . . ." In the third sonnet of "The Womanhood," *(Annie Allen)* those who believe in the religious simplicities are "metaphysical mules" (stubborn), and the black mother, in her compassion, stands ready to sew up the children's assaulted beliefs, "Holding the bandage ready for your eyes." Interestingly, this image of the merciful blindfold appears in her first volume of poetry *(A Street in Bronzeville,* 1945) in "the funeral," and in the same volume the women in "Satin Legs Smith" wend their way from "service," with "Temperate holiness arranged ably on asking faces. . . ."

It is true that Miss Brooks ended the over-anthologized poem "The Chicago Defender Sends a Man to Little Rock" with the line "The loveliest lynchee was our Lord" *(The Bean Eaters),* but she now rejects the line, and feels that Blacks are the true figures on the Cross. It is also true that she wrote a poem on the second coming of Christ, "In Emanuel's Nightmare: Another Coming of Christ," but here Christ is more of a cultural fact than a passionate commitment. Christ is present largely to project man's pitiful commitment to the dirtiness of war. Other poems might be cited. But perhaps the foregoing will suffice to suggest that, whereas Miss Brooks evidences a very deep religious consciousness, her commitment over the years to the idea of Christianity has been neither simple nor unquestioning.

The same judgment applies to the simplicity of Miss Brooks's statement that she had believed persistent appeals to whites for help would gain meaningful responses. Like many people, Miss Brooks has probably had periods of euphoric confidence in the effectiveness of "education" in race relations, shored up by individual interracial friendships, but also periods and intervals of gnawing doubt and teeth gritting frustration out of which her present sense of the implacability of institutionalized racism grew. I have already referred to the stern ambivalence of "Negro Hero" (1945). "The Sundays of Satin-Legs Smith" reflects both a compassionate and a skeptical attitude toward the white "you" whom she is addressing. "I Love those little booths at Benvenuti's," *(Annie Allen)* and "The Lovers of the Poor" *(The Bean Eaters)* range in tone from cool signifying to sustained and slashing attack. In other poems published prior to 1968, there are also an in-between mildness and a variety of modulations.

At any rate, whites repeatedly called her bitter and asked whether she didn't think things were changing. Many hated *The Bean Eaters*. Miss Brooks, in the Stavros interview, refers to their dislike of "Lovers of the Poor" and of so mild a poem as "The Chicago Defender Sends a Man to Little Rock: Fall, 1957."[16]

On both issues of religion and race, Prof. Arthur P. Davis felt that "She doesn't seem to have much faith in either the American Dream or a Just God."[17]

Phyl Garland's passages on the childhood and growing up years of Miss Brooks give further insight into her sensibility.[18] On the one hand, she is the dreamy child who, by the age of seven, was finding happiness in reading and writing. Her greatest happiness came as she stood upon the neat patch of physical, cultural, and spiritual ground won by the quiet but determined devotion of her parents, and gazed upon the changeful beauty of the clouds—a day-dream analogy of the beauty she desired for her future. Miss Garland points out that the adventure with clouds meant seeing beyond the "grimy, tottering back stairs of a row of tenements" facing the Brooks's backyard. On the other hand, between the ages of thirteen and twenty, Miss Brooks had published two neighborhood newspapers, *The Champlain Weekly News* and the *News Review,* a fact which evidences an intense interest in people and their doings.[19] When combined, her activities seem to predict her fascination with the people's vitality, beauty, horror, pathos, and inchoate yearnings, reflected in her published poetry, and her strong commitment to neighborhood and community.

One notices the number of poems which are derived and transformed from specific real life situations: "The Vacant Lot," "Matthew Cole," "The Murder," "Obituary for a Living Lady," "A Song in the Front Yard" (autobiographically based), the World War II poems "Gay Chaps at the Bar," parts of *Annie Allen,* the situation and certain characters of "In the Mecca," friends and historical figures in *In the Mecca* and *Family Pictures.*[20] To these might be added, in poetry, carefully observed types such as Satin Legs Smith, and in fiction, characters of the partly autobiographical novel *Maud Martha.* Miss Brooks kept a notebook and, at one time, jotted down observations in restaurants and other public places.[21] The total situation highlights the fact that her poetry is peopled-centered, and that she makes very strong cases for them.

One other aspect of sensibility stemming from childhood seems inescapable: her experience of an unwanted awkwardness and separateness from other children, black and white (outside her neighborhood), caused by shyness, lack of the usual childhood skill, intra —and interracial prejudice, and her unusual interests. Her sense of at-homeness in her neighborhood and her imaginative sympathies were a partial compensation. But the more formal social barriers in school set her apart. Thus the issues of intra-racial prejudice crop up in her poetry sufficiently to rival, in quantity, her preoccupation with interracial prejudice. On the intra-racial level, her experience with prejudice against a black skin and preference for the light skin began in grammar school, as can be seen in the poem "The Ballad of Chocolate Mabbie,"[22] and in a section of her novel *Maude Martha*. On the interracial situation, she could say that at Hyde Park Branch High School "I wasn't so much injured, just left alone. I realized that they were a society apart, and they really made you feel it. None of them [whites] would have anything to do with you, aside from some white boy if he fell in love with you."[23]

Miss Brooks's sensibility then comprises powerful negatives and positives. In the poetry we find them yoked and coordinated—a source of deep compassion and empathy reflected both in the strength of the cases she makes for her people and the sudden appearances of the author's own voice, as in this part from "The Sundays of Satin Legs Smith":

> People are so in need, in need of help.
> People want so much that they do not know.
>
> Below the tinkling trade of little coins
> The gold impulse not possible to show
> Or spend. Promise piled over and betrayed.

This voice surges forward wherever misery and frustration challenge beauty and vitality and can be heard powerfully in such a poem as "In the Mecca." It also comes forth, at times, in incisive and slashing attacks.

It is this powerful sensibility which has caused the poet to invest her energies in assistance to her community and in a poetry which has resulted in formal recognitions which would require several pages to list. Her community activities are in such categories as financing and awarding numerous prizes in poetry and the arts; sponsorships of contests and workshops on all school levels and in the community; direct assistance to artists; teaching and lecturing; and editing a magazine soon to appear under the title *Black Position.*[24]

She has won an elaborate array of prizes for poetry within the State of Illinois, and regionally, and nationally. Within Illinois she is State Poet Laureate and, on the national scene, holder of the Pulitzer Prize for *Annie Allen.* From academic areas, there are two Guggenheim awards and a dozen academic honorary degrees. In September 1971, supplementing other academic posts, is her appointment as Visiting Professor at the College of the City of New York. From the black community, there are the formal and public testimonial of 1969 in Chicago and a book of poems written by younger and mature black authors in tribute to her personality and works entitled *To Gwen With Love,* 1971.

What should be clear so far is that her sensibility produces a unified confontation with life and art, and that, in rendering the black experience she can be said to be out real far on its perilous seas and in real deep.

I turn now to analyses of specific poems, some of which are known as "difficult."

III

Among the shorter poems, I should like to move under the broad classifications of light and complex. My use of the term "light" does not carry a connotation of inferiority, but means that the author is deliberately refraining from making a complete investigation of a heavyweight emotion or fully occupying and rendering all vibrations and space the theme and subject may be capable of yielding. By complex, I mean that the poem is after the illusion of full occupation of the subject's possibilities and space, and full rendering of vibrations—contradictory or otherwise.

Although she may mean something different by it, Miss Brooks, herself, has used the term "light" in referring to such a work as "A Song in the Front Yard," and the expression "very simple little thing" in referring to "A Light and Diplomatic Bird."[25] The latter, she says, is not to be compared to a poem like "Kitchenette Building," since its subject is a girl merely temporarily overwhelmed by grief. An important enough subject, of course, but, I presume, in its emotional preoccupations, not of the sweep and depth of the people of "Kitchenette Building" who are under the threat of permanent estrangement from the right to dream and aspire.

"A Song in the Front Yard," expresses the child speaker's desire to escape the highly ordered and somewhat devitalized life of her front yard training for the wild vitality of the back. It gains its legitimacy from the autonomy that mature adults would wish to grant childhood feelings, without yielding to a child's logic. The child identifies with the raw vitality of life, an identity which the adult also reveres but controls in the name of an ordered society. But Miss Brooks presents simply the poignant view of the child.

The same principle applies to such a poem as "Sadie and Maude," which celebrates confrontation with the raw and rich vitality of life—and the mastering of it by Sadie with her fine tooth comb which she leaves as a heritage to her daughter. It would be rather stuffy of the reader to point out that the Sadies and their daughters don't seem to have the final answer either, since they often run into deadly traps and leave great debts for the brown mouse Maudes to pay. The poet is content to suggest the possibility of a higher wisdom on the part of the Sadies and to celebrate the vitality of life. Miss Brooks, who lives today in a vital community on South Evans Street, Chicago, at one time lived in a rawer area, and many of the better known poems derive from it—623 East 63rd Street, in a second floor apartment where discussions with her husband were sometimes interrupted by an elevated train ("That comes on like a slightly horrible thought.") and she could look from one side of the street to the other: "There was my material."[26]

Other examples of poems that might be included in the "light" category are: "the preacher ruminates behind the sermon," a poem ostensibly about God but which might be applied to others who hold high isolated positions; "the independent man," a poem satirizing the egocentric male; "the vacant lot," a satirical piece on adulterous and prideful behavior; "Sunday Chicken," a poem lightly satirical of man's residual cannibalism; and "pygamies are pygamies still, though percht on Alps," a satrical piece on the pretensions of the great.

Regarding the more complex poems, I shall begin with the negative, and suggest reasons why some pieces do not completely fulfill themselves. "the mother" seems to me to protest too much and to suffer from a labored irony, which fails to convey the attitude of the author toward her subject—the several abortions of the mother. Thus on the poetic scales the mixture of irony and compassion settles into the merely sentimental. "The Queen of the Blues," an interesting poem that adventures with ballad and blues form, finally needs stronger symbols more in line with the gritty uncertanties of the old time blues life. If one may trust autobiographies of women blues singers, the pinching of their arms and slapping of their thighs were among the *minor* evils lurking in the entertainment jungle, which the singers learned to deal with (or endure) long before they became queens. The life, itself, seems hardly to fit in with the frame of standard chilvaric tradition suggested by the singer's hunger for a tipped hat. Perhaps Langston Hughes's term, "a do right man," would convey the idea of the singer's need more effectively. In such poems (both from *A Street in Bronzeville*) Miss Brooks seems to be dealing, not with the life of such a personality as would probably arise from known circumstances, but with a generous extension of her own values. One gets the feeling that the sensibility did not really encompass the realities of the subject. "The Ballad of Pearl May Lee," an attack upon black boys seduced by white girls, does not seem suited to standard ballad form and devices, and the jumping and lilting movement of the poem seems to go too far in avoiding real confrontation with the black girl's emotions.

Similar problems, it seems to me, hover close by or to some degree entrap parts of most Southern located poems. I refer to such poems as "A Bronzeville Mother Loiters in MISSISSIPPI, MEANWHILE, A MISSISSIPPI MOTHER BURNS BACON," and the much anthologized "THE CHICAGO DEFENDER SENDS A MAN TO LITTLE ROCK."

The vibrations of history and culture push hard upon such poems, making one wish to understand particulars, and Miss Brooks seems to arrive at the universal a bit too soon. "A BRONZEVILLE MOTHER—" is obviously inspired by the lynching of Emmett "Bobo" Till, a fourteen-year-old Chicago black boy who was brutally destroyed and dumped into a Mississippi river because he allegedly made "advances" to a young white woman in a Mississippi cross-roads store in the summer of 1955. Miss Brooks examines the responses of a similar white woman, after the trial, using the framework of ballad and chilvaric tradition. The white woman plays the role of "the milk-white maid," the 'maid mild'/of the [traditional] ballad. Pursued/by the Dark Villain. . . ." After a sense of exaltation in her role, it finally (and simply) occurs to her that the traditional Dark Villain was really a mere child "with eyes still too young to be dirty" and a mouth not yet bereft of "every reminder/ of its infant softness." A succession of domestic scenes follow, in which the vengeful husband reveals by brutality to his children that he is not at all the Fine Prince. Within the woman "a hatred for him burst into glorious flowers." Now the pressure of public and historical knowledge of such lynch situations is that they were rituals through which white Southern women of almost any "moral" condition were instantly transformed into Miss Southern White Woman, and that the rhythms of Southern culture and tradition arose to absorb their "conscience" in the "conscience of the community."

Now I'm not saying anything so simple-minded as "no Southern white woman could have had such feelings." As a matter of fact, one version of the real life situation and woman is that the woman, herself, did not report the "advances" to her husband, a possibility which might well have given the poet her cue for portraying the character of the poem. It was said that the offended husband received the report from some of the local Negroes. My point, rather, is that where cultural and historical circumstances press a counter image upon the mind, the artist must show greater strain and struggle before the simple universal woman's heart emerges. It is a matter of the power of artistic illusion.

Basically, the same judgment is called for regarding "The Chicago DEFENDER SENDS A MAN TO LITTLE ROCK," a poem inspired by the very bitter and literally nasty outbreak of violence against young black boys and girls when mobs in Little Rock, Arkansas, attempted to prevent desegregation of schools. As in the preceding poem, there are brilliant lines and mastery of the homely detail. The poem contains a kind of truth—but one not sufficiently dramatized against the city's cultural context. Little Rock arrives at the universal by a quick strip-tease of its cultural clothing, and by immediate emphasis upon what it shares in common with others. Thus we light upon the universal: "They are like people everywhere."

But the foregoing poems are aberrations and deviations from a usually brilliant performance, in which the illusion is rendered that the last word has been said upon the subject. In "Sundays of Satin-Legs Smith," for example, the balance seems everywhere just right and is the deepest study of the hip style and the significance of the now old-time zoot-suiter. The poems builds upon a basic five beat line and makes use of many of the poet's brilliant resources—minglings of poetic attitudes, the finely turned phrase which delights and surprises, the interesting use of adjectives and unusual juxtaposition of words, and a just balance between the formal eloquence and the colloquial. A good example of the last mentioned resource is in the following short verse:

> He wakes, unwinds, elaborately: a cat
> Tawny, reluctant, royal. He is fat
> And fine this morning.   Definite.   Reimbursed.

The poet renders all Smith's glamor and brilliance, but a misery in his surroundings and in his fellow men and a blindness within Smith, himself, indites everything—including the society which produced him. We are, therefore, not served up the usual small minded glamor concerning the hip posture.

> The pasts of his ancestors lean against
> Him. Crowd him. Fog out his identity.
> Hundreds of hungers mingle with his own,
> Hundreds of voices advise so dexterously
> He quite considers his reactions his,
> Judges he walks most powerfully alone,
> That everything is—simply what it is.

The poem has intervals for such touches, and manages to move from the suggestion of heroic stance to the pathetic.

"The parents: people like our marriage, Maxie and Andrew," is a portrait of a kind of striving that gains while really losing everything. It is interesting for its use of simple symbols: swans and swallows for the richness, nobleness and grace of life; chicken, porches, prim low fencing, and pleasant custards, for surrender to a deadly material nothingness. Thus it has an irony which is pervasive and whose dramatic fire blazes or lies banked, depending upon the values of the reader. The contrast is sharp: What is lost from the eyes and the people is all the value that we associate with "the light that bites or terrifies." Thus the highly concentrated beginning, "Clogged and soft and sloppy eyes," represents in brilliant drama those who fled the Great Adventure and settled for a bland comfort. Every symbol works—the "prim low fencing pinching in the grass" makes of the imprisoned grass a thing of many associations. Finally, since there is not space to quote the entire poem, the poet is revealed as the master of the great and grand line which simply grows still grander in its teamwork with the rest of the poem.

> Clogged and soft and sloppy eyes
> Have lost the light that bites or terrifies.

It is this type of poem which inexorably occupies its entire space and gives the illusion of saying the last word upon the subject. Now some will see the poem in terms of "transcending," but it really goes down deep for its universal. Beneath its failure to mention race is the description of a black style which is also traditional.

Miss Brooks's sonnets are also interesting for their digging in. I have attempted to describe their varied style and will take up here only Sonnet II of the series "the children of the poor." It happens to be the most masterly statement of the dilemma of the black mother in poetry and, in the sestet, one of the more memorable movements and rhythmic developments in the English language. The first eight lines are an elaborate, complex, but incisive question. What shall the mother give her children who are poor, devalued, loved (by the mother) outcasts (sweetest lepers), questing for no softness but a definite profile, from an imperfect hand. They are unfinished, contraband. In the poem, Blackness is nowhere mentioned, but the outcast status and the agony of the mother should make the situation perfectly clear. In the sestet, the mother firmly faces her tragedy as she describes it and the words are chosen both for nuance and for full tragic tone:

> My hand is stuffed with mode, design, device
> But I lack access to my proper stone.
> And plenitude of plan shall not suffice
> Nor grief nor love shall be enough alone
> To ratify my little halves who bear
> Across an autumn freezing everywhere.

I think that the "stone" in the second line should be interpreted as philosopher's stone, an imaginary substance once thought capable of turning plain metal to gold. Again, we have genuine universalism arrived at by a deep plumbing of the mother's situation.

For other of the shorter, complex poems, a few may be selected and brief explications must suffice. Sonnet III deals with the mother's confrontation with the inadequacy of religion, moves densely, but ends with a line that seems somewhat clumsy and literal—and therefore a bit out of tone with the preceding lines. "do not be afraid of no" is full of brilliant and dramatic language emphasizing the necessity to stand firmly upon one's own feet, face the pain of life in order to make it meaningful, and to avoid all death bestowing compromises. The rough and abrupt movement and tone of the poem fits the mood of stern self-advice, and should be clear so long as it is realized that the lines in quotation marks are addressed to the self. (I thought, at first, that they were quoted from a poem by the 19th Century poet, Emily Dickinson, but was corrected by Miss Brooks.)

"Strong Men, Riding Horses: Lester after the Western" is a tight drama contrasting the movies showing the "bravery" of the Western cowboys with the done-in squirmings of a rent-paying viewer who in a climactic line confesses, "I am not brave at all." The poem's simplicity is deceptive. Actually the poet, in highly concentrated expressions first exposes the stage phoniness of the cowboys, who come with a ready-made posture of being "pasted to the stars already." The broad chests are those of the Hollywood actor, and the actors are saddled for the production of illusion. We recall that the cowboys have simple concrete villains. Lester has "illegible landlords" to battle, that is, faceless opponents, and robbers. Against the assaults that come daily from modern life (daily dues paying), Lester must have *mouths* to "word-wall off that broadness of the dark. . . ." Thus, Lester, though indeed pitiful, represents a reality, whereas the cowboys do not. "A Lovely Love" celebartes the insistent assertion of itself by love, although it lacks the proper stage since it lacks the "swaddling clothes," "fondling star," and "wise men" surrounding the birth of Christ. Thus, though it must assert itself secretly in slum hallways, on stairways, and remain "definitionless," in the strict atmosphere of convention, its existence is its triumph.

I approach "Riders to the Blood Red Wrath" *(Selected Poems)* assisted by a paraphrase made by Miss Brooks and some extensions of my own. In reading the poem, the reader will place himself to advantage by seeing the attack as made by freedom riders, the sit-ins, the wade-ins, etc., all the pushers for "what is reliably right." In the first stanza, the segregationists and oppressors generally are astonished by the new behavior of persons insisting upon their rights, which they regard as outside the realms of decorum. The language is concentrated to suggest the complexity of emotion of the attackers, insisting upon their rights. The oppressors refuse to understand the complex fury of the oppressed and oppose it by traditions, which are death refusing to acknowledge the rebirth of its victims.

In the second stanza, the oppressed, imbued still with the "stated principles" of America, fight boldly but in a controlled and restricted fashion. Under the control is rage and justified resentment. This rage is "my guns" sewed . . . "inside my burning lips." The charger, "my fury," has pushed forward the softer horse," the mare which does the "official talking," but it is not as mild as it looks.[27] Still the act of apparent mildness has caused the enemy to commit all sorts of crimes against man and God.

Stanza 4 indicates both the bearing up under unforgivable injustices and a new strength and determination and knowledge which prevent injustices from "sticking daily in the craw" as they once did. Along with this new strength is the remembrance of the vitality and freedom of Africa. In stanzas five and six, the Black's side of the slave trade is remembered and slavery, subjugation, and "criminal reduction." In stanza seven, the movement is toward utilizing one's own suffering which enables Blacks to see man's general inhumanity. This inhumanity runs loose everywhere.

In stanzas 8 and 9, the realization of universal cruelty strengthens the Blacks and develops a determination to revere, esteem and respect what is human. Thus the poet can say, "Democracy and Christianity/Recommence with me." And thus the determination to struggle persistently in the interest of love ("in the larger sense"), whether to result in failure or in victory. Therefore, the words that described the determination: "We lurch, distribute, we extend, begin."

Once the general framework is grasped, the poem will be seen to contain the philosophy of the non-violent movement and express its courage.

Since 1967, Miss Brooks's poetry, however, has incorporated the tensions of the time that saw disillusionment arise from the struggle for integration. Shorter poems in *In the Mecca, Riot,* and *Family Pictures,* reflect the pressing urgency of the post-integration tensions. They render, without polemics, a call upon the community to recognize itself and a celebration of the newer personalities— hopefully a race of men arriving to take control. Then there are celebrations in which the black community may simply be made more conscious of its own qualities, values, and complexities.

The bridge to the newer poems is possibly the poem "Medgar Evers," which celebrates the achievement and stance of the Mississippi NAACP leader who was cut down by the bullets of a white assassin. The poem has kinship with "Riders,"—but states its point in more direct though concentrated language. It begins:

> "The man whose height his fear improved he
> arranged to fear not further. The raw
> intoxicated time was time for better birth or
> a final death.

The stance of Medgar Evers is to attack tradition, produce irritation, and to "lean across tomorrow," in order to present a new and redeemed world "People said he was holding clean globes in his hands."

"The Wall" of August 27, 1957, is a celebration within the strict emotions of the black group as it confronts an implacable racism and respects its own sense of unity and togetherness. Here the poet appears as a part of the embattled community. It should perhaps be explained that "The Wall" is the Wall of Respect, exhibiting paintings on a building at 43rd and Langley, Chicago, which pictures black heroes who have been meaningful in the life of the community. It represents a rejection of all former dispensations which have left Blacks enslaved and impoverished amidst a world of plenty.

> On Forty-third and Langley
> black furnaces resent ancient
> legislatures
> of ploy and scruple and practical gelatin
> They keep the fever in,
> fondle the fever.

If "The Wall" represents an identification of the poet with her people and a celebration of various matters important to the group, the three sermons on the warpland (America), reveal her spiritual commitment. The first two *(In the Mecca)* acknowledge a new condition of black people and summon them to the pain and exhaltation of destruction and new birth. In Sermon I, the first five lines record a new stance toward the American "mainstream" (the River). The rest of the poem deals with the fall of old idols, the promise of new health and new vision which must result in creation through a new and powerful love.

> Say that our Something in doublepod contains
> seeds for the coming hell and health together.
> Prepare to meet
> (sisters, brothers) the brash and terrible weather,
> the pains,
> the bruising; the collapse of bestials, idols,
> But then oh then!—the stuffing of the hulls!

Sermon II is even more intense in facing the chaos out of which the new must come. It urges people to stand up and live during the process: "This is the urgency. Live!/ and have your blooming in the noise of the whirlwind." Section IV of the sermon mounts powerfully to a climax and the language matches a high point of the wave of the new explosive black radical movement:

The time
cracks into furious flower. Lifts its face
all unashamed. And sways in wicked grace.
Whose half-black hands assemble oranges
is tom-tom hearted
(goes in bearing oranges and boom)
And there are bells for orphans—
and red and shriek and sheen.
A garbageman is dignified
as any diplomat.
Big Bessie's feet hurt like nobody's business,
but she stands—bigly—under the unruly scrutiny, stands in
    the wild weed.

The Third Sermon continues the commitment and deals more directly with rebellion scenes and their significance *(Riot,* 1969.)

It would be well to read *In the Mecca, Riot,* and *Family Pictures* together, since they stand as a unit in representing the poet's responsiveness to the black community's changing vibrations and attempts to recreate itself. As we shall see, the long poem "In the Mecca" gives a background of the deadend urban life (radical voices can already be heard within it) which created the new black movement. The shorter poems in *In the Mecca, Riot,* and *Family Pictures* register both the surging new vision of Blacks and, particularly in *Family Pictures,* a deep reflection of those new values for the living and "blooming in the noise and whip of the whirlwind." In the process, what one discovers for himself and about the poet is the ever deepening and varied swells of her seas. This discovery of varied depths, as if she always has more banked and damned-in waters to deal with, is certain if the reader then goes back to visit among the depths of her earlier works.

And it remains now to turn briefly to "The Anniad" and "In the Mecca" for some examples of the complexity of the poet in the longer forms. What falls by the wayside at once is any generalization about the poet's being at home only in the shorter form. Not that "The Anniad" is wholly successful, but there is sufficient success to make it the deepest poem in literature to deal with the life of a young black woman. Nikki Giovanni, herself a radical poet, strikes the exact note in "For Gwen Brooks from Nikki Giovanni":

". . . and Annie Allen and I met. And it flowed. And titillated and teased and made me feel. And I didn't like to feel. And I understood Annie Allen to be my mother and I sympathized with her and loved her."[28]

"The Anniad," of course, represents the girlhood and young womanhood of Annie Allen, who gives the book its title, and there are many poems covering other phases of Annie Allen's life. But certainly "The Anniad" is one of those poems which you feel before fully understanding the nuances. In discussing the main drifts of the poem, I speak with assistance from Miss Brooks (also true of "In the Mecca), but absolve her from responsibility for any errors.

The first five stanzas render the beauty of a young woman reveling in her own flowering into maturity and consequent dreams of fulfillment through and with the dream man. The feelings are expressed through a tension between the shape of dreams derived from nature and chilvaric tradition and the black girl's unacknowledged and peculiar stance in the halls of chivalry. For suddenly she bursts forth with the famous lines:

> Think of thaumaturgic lass
> Looking in her looking-glass
> at the unembroidered brown;
> Printing bastard roses there;
> Then emotionally aware
> Of the black and boisterous hair,
> Taming all that anger down.

There is no single verse or poem which as brilliantly sums up the conflict which a black woman could feel before the natural hair movement made some moderation of the necessity to keep one eye focused upon white standards of beauty.

The next six stanzas portray the courtship and early married life between Annie Allen and "a man of tan." The stanzas subtly portray the ritual games by which the young woman pretends to defend so that the Prince will invade, and the descent into a realism without immediately abandoning dreams or sacred efforts to create a universe. The diction is, therefore, religious: "hot theopathy," "nun of crimson ruses," the home as "chapel," "genuflects to love," "prayerbooks in her eyes," etc. Also continued—some language from the tradition of courtly love. The sharply realistic elements, however, reside in the desperate but skilled effort of the young woman to turn the "lowly room" the man leads her to into a proper stage for the grandeur of love, to escape "grayness" and existence without definition. (Compare "A Lovely Love," *Selected Poems.)*

Into this barely propped Eden breaks World War II. The next twelve stanzas carry us through the war service, the return of a diseased husband, his post-War maladjustments which wreck the marriage. The husband is the soldier estranged by war experiences whose taut emotions now finds neither commensurate rewards in civilian life nor a continuation of his fragile hero status. As a black man, he is quickly trapped, finds his wife little compensation and turns for consolation to a light-skinned woman (maple banshee). His rejection of his wife is expressed in the following stanza:

> Not that woman! Not that room!
> Not that dusted demi gloom
> Nothing limpid, nothing meek.
> But a gorgeous and gold shriek
> With her tongue tucked in her cheek,
> Hissing gauzes in her gaze,
> Coiling oil upon her ways.

The next twelve stanzas begin with the refrain' "Think of Sweet Chocolate" and end with the stanza beginning, "Perfumes fly before the gust . . ." They cover a period which involves the young woman's turning to inadequate compensations for the loss of her husband. She turns to nature, friends, books, romance, and children, but finds only that:

> Perfumes fly before the gust,
> Colors shrivel in the dust,
> And the petal velvet shies
> When the dessert terrifies
> Howls, revolves, and countercharms:
> Shakes its great and gritty arms;
> And perplexes with odd eyes.

The rest of the poem portrays the fatally war diseased husband abandoning his mistress, returning to his devoted wife to die, and the wife gathering together her shattered life and memories after his death. Her final situation is expressed in the last stanza.

> Think of almost thoroughly
> Derelict and dim and done.
> Stroking swallows from the sweat.
> Fingering faint violet,
> Hugging old and Sunday sun.
> Kissing in her kitchenette
> The minuets of memory.

I shall not attempt an elaborate explication, since the many stanzas would require a separate article, but suffice it to say that once the main lines of development are grasped the stanzas yield their meaning easily to close attention and produce considerable excitement. The poem justifies its epic title, and the warm glow and changes the woman goes through are powerfully suggested by use of language which has deep connotations drawn from chivalry, religion, music, nature, general classical tradition, the military, and black life. The kitchenette setting, as in other poems of the poet, drives home the fact that life's inevitable sweep of misery, beauty, and the tragic, demand a place in the heart of being whether or not the grand and gilted symbols and stage can be arranged to grace the drama. The poet has seized upon the great truth that the area of the fulfilled life is a battle ground which makes little fellows of both cowards and "heroes." Even if one meets the situation with resourceful energy and brief postures of the upright stance, the probability is an outcome not too far distant from Satin Legs Smith or Lester After the Western or, in the case before us, the resourceful Annie somewhat redeeming the time by "Stroking swallows from the sweat . . ." and ". . . Kissing in her kitchenette/ The minuets of memory."

Looking from "The Anniad" backward and forward over the body of Miss Brooks's poetry, we can now see that she has made the subject, the tragic struggle for fulfillment without the illusion-giving stage and rituals validated and dignified by tradition, peculiarly her own. In a sense, it also defines the Blackness of her poetry —the harsh bare stage and lineless scenes being qualities so often characterizing the struggle of black life in the modern city—thus part of the terrifying beauty of Annie derives from the sections covering her dreams and her illusioned attempt to force upon her marriage a defining stage. From there on, circumstances inexorably take over, as they do their ghoulish dance. My main quibble with the poem is an unfulfilled desire to see more deeply into the husband and an encounter with a few stanzas that are greater as performance than as communication.

We may fittingly end with a discussion of the pre-revolutionary long poem, "In the Mecca," since it contains powerful strands of both the earlier and later period of the poet's creativity. The prose background facts of the actual building entitled "The Mecca" may be gained from the article in the December, 1950 issue of *Harper's* Magazine, "The Strangest Place in Chicago," by John Bartlow Martin.[29] Before it was demolished, it was a building, four stories high, "topped by an ungainly smokestack, ancient and enormous, filling half the block north of 34th Street between State and Dearborn." Constructed as a showplace apartment building in 1891, it was a U-shaped building with four main entrances, "two on Dearborn and two on State Street." By 1950, the building, which began deteriorating during the World War I period and underwent usage first by whites, then by a variety of types of Blacks, had become "one of the most remarkable slum exhibits in the world." The number of people occupying the building in 1950 was variously estimated: 1400, over 2,000, 2300. Nobody really knew. One man reported that the building contained 176 apartments, "some with seven rooms and they're all full." Another that people would be found "sleeping in bathtubs, sleeping in the kitchen under the sink, anywhere they can sleep." By 1950 all but one of the occupants were black, the overwhelming number poor although there were some holdovers from earlier days. It was a building where the kinds of violence, exploitation, filthy conditions, and misery, associated with slums, abounded.

Thus for Miss Brooks the building could stand as a symbol of that narrow space in which urban Blacks acted out their measure of heroism, misery, and love—all the problems of human fulfillment ungraced by the grand stage. It could also reflect the general misery abroad in the world.

Her proposal for the poem stated that:[30] "I wish to present a large variety of personalities against a mosaic of daily affairs, recognizing that the grimmest of these is likely to have a streak or two of sun." The proposal also speaks of the effort to "capsule the gist of black humanity in general."

The story and structure are very simple. Mrs. Sallie Smith, the mother of nine children awaiting her return from the day's work for affluent whites, comes home to find all her children in their habitual preoccupations, except the young Pepita. Mrs. Sallie and her children unsuccessfully search the building for her. A policeman finally finds her dead under the cot of Jamaican Edward with the roaches. But so bald a summary gives no idea of the depth and power of the poem. It is concerned with rendering the deep insights into the frustrated occupants and displaying Pepita as the destroyed beautiful child, symbol of an uncaring world. Most personalities are re-enforced in their position as souls in isolation by the crowding upon them of an unlovely society.

Two personalities are introduced to us by having Mrs. Sallie pass their apartments on her way to her own—old St. Julia, who has retreated into a religious ecstasy which makes of God "an incense and a vitage"; and Alfred, the frustrated intellectual and would-be writer (who might have been an architect or poet-king), who risks losing himself in sex and drink. His voice forms part of the interpreting chorus. Miss Brooks strikes her note with him very early.

> Sallie sees Alfred. Ah, his God!—
> To create! To create! To bend with the right intentness
> over the neat detail, come to
> a terrified standstill of the heart, then shiver,
> then rush—successfully—
> at that rebuking thing, that obstinate and
> recalcitrant little beast, the phrase!
>
> • • •
>
> Alfred is un-
> talented. Knows. Marks time and themes at Phillips,
> stares, glares, of mornings, at a smear
> which does not care what he may claim or doubt
> or probe or clear or want, or what he might have been.
>
> • • •

is weak, is no good. Never mind
It is a decent enough no-goodness. And it is a
talkative, curly, charitable, spiced weakness
which makes a woman in charge of zoology
dream furiously at night.

I have had to cut the first long passage, but the excerpt gives also
an idea of the incisive analysis applied to him and others.

As Mrs. Sallie enters her apartment, we have the stage set for
portrayal of atmosphere and introduction of her children. Mrs.
Sallie has brought hock of ham, six ruddy yams, and will make corn-
bread with water. But she is disgusted with her kitchen, a fact
which the poet express partly in the language of formal eloquence.

Her denunciation
slaps savagely not only this sick kitchen but
her Lord's annulment of the main event.
"I want to decorate!" But what is that? A
pomade atop a sewage. An offense,
First comes correctness, *then* embellishment!
And music, mode, and mixed philosophy
may follow fitly on propriety
to name the whiskey of our discontent!

The children have striking qualities and are, in varying degrees,
in isolation with their preoccupations. Several exist among uneasy
tensions which might at any time destroy them: Yvonne, uneasy
over her lover; Melodie Mary, delicate and with deep sympathy for
rats; Briggs, "adult as a stone," who must come to terms with gangs.
Others have various issues to confront, but all show a sharp intelli-
gence. After introducing all children, the poet uses Alfred, as a
chorus to comment upon the world's betraying its holy duties, and
suddenly Mrs. Sallie discovers the absence of Pepita.

The resulting tour takes us among several personalities who
are incisively and suggestively analyzed, presented. They, sometimes
reveal a secret beauty or a twisted and lugubrious charm or a deep
misery. The more aware personalities, such as Loam Norton provide an opportunity to deepen the sense of misery abroad in the
world, Norton by a bitter parody of the 21st Psalm: "The Lord was

their [residents of Belsen and Duchau] shepherd,/yet did they want. . . ." Aunt Dill heightens the agony by telling of a little girl who was choked and raped last week, obviously enjoying the gory details. Another provides a picture of obsessive revolutionary commitment—but without much plan. Actual personalities, such as the poet Don L. Lee, provide the note of black nationhood. Thus the story is a mixture of atmosphere, events, insights into personalities, and the historical misery of Blacks, along with the general misery of mankind. Added to these are the choruses, those given in the voice of the author being the most beautiful. She ends the poem on the fate of Pepita, dead under the bed of Jamaican Eddie.

> a little woman lies in dust with roaches.
> She never went to kindergarten.
> She never learned that black is not beloved,
> Was royalty when poised,
> sly, at the A and P's fly-open door.
> Will be royal no more.
> "I touch"—she said once—"petals of a rose.
> A silky feeling through me goes!"
> She whose little stomach fought the world had
> wriggled, like a robin!
> Odd were the little wrigglings
> and the chopped chirpings oddly rising.

Like "The Anniad" of *Annie Allen,* "In the Mecca" deserves its own separate analysis, but perhaps this brief presentation will suggest its depths, its full occupation of its imaginative space, its complete projection and enclosure of all vibrations belonging to its situation. The remainder of the volume is fittingly placed under the heading of "After Mecca," since the succeeding poems deal largely with the coming whirlwind sown in the Mecca. One may indeed say, After Mecca, what forgiveness? A multitude of radical poems by young radical Blacks have followed and attempted to give the answer.

To paraphrase a remark Miss Brooks made on a different occasion: the poem maintains a just balance between private suffusion and public clamor. With its elaborate choral arrangements, its free verse experimentations and complete command of the incisive line, its easy movement between the colloquial and formal eloquence, and arrangements for historical sweep, it becomes one of those very terrible wastelands that jump forth with vitality at each reading. And Miss Brooks's would-be poet-intellectual-king-architect does not allow us to forget its terrible human imperative.

> I hate it.
> Yet, murmurs Alfred—
> who is lean at the balcony, leaning—
> something, something in Mecca
> continues to call! Substanceless; yet like mountains,
> like rivers and oceans too; and like trees
> with wind whistling through them. And steadily
> an essential sanity, black and electric,
> builds to a reportage and redemption.
>> A hot estrangement.
>> A material collapse
> that is Construction.

It should not be surprising, therefore, to discover that the only comparable work operating in the very depths of black blues in the city is Richard Wright's novel, *Native Son*.

And now what is to be said concerning the body of the poetry highlighted here? It certainly places the poet on the front row of the platform containing any rigorous selection of black writers who have written in America. Although she lacks the facility possessed by such writers as Langston Hughes and Margaret Walker to move directly into the Southern past, she provides an intensity of suggestion which makes the past terribly alive in a terrible present.

But there is an additional matter which other critics might well ponder. Those who claim that the black experience is but another part of the American experience must then work through the rigor of their logic. If they can recognize the powerful meaning of the black experience in America, and if they can absent themselves briefly from a general contemporary American poetry which so often ranges between a dry intellectuality and abstruse claims from the individual psyche, then Miss Brooks must rise very high in their measurements. And, if a people-centered poetry can then exert a claim, they must place her within the roughly baker's dozen of truly significant poets writing in America during the 20th Century.

But the arrival at such a judgment, implies the stance called for in the great opening lines of "In the Mecca."

> Sit where the light corrupts your face.
> Mies Van der Rohe retires from grace.
> And the fair fables fall.

Reprinted from *Black World*, September, 1971

FOOTNOTES

1 The impact of the radical movement can be seen in her poetry, and in the following descriptions: Phyl Garland, "Gwendolyn Brooks: Poet Laureate," *Ebony*, 23 (July, 1968), pp. 48 & 49, passim: Ida Lewis, "Conversation," *Essence*, April, 1971, p. 27; George Stavros, "An Interview With Gwendolyn Brooks," *Contemporary Literature*, 11 (Winter, 1970), pp. 5-7; *We Asked Gwendolyn Brooks*, u.d., Illinois Bell Telephone, passim.
2. See Stavros, for example, pp. 10-11, passim. (Also stated to me in Interview.)
3. Stavros, p. 10.
4. *Ibid.*
5. Stavros, p. 12. Other quotations on the page also from Stavros.
6. Lewis, p. 28.
7. *Ibid.*
8. Herbert Hill, *Soon One Morning* (New York, 1963), p. 326. The book contains also the first version of the piece "The Life of Lincoln West," now with slight changes to heighten poetic effect reprinted in *Family Pictures*.
9. Glenda Estelle Clyde, *An Oral Interpreter's Approach to the Poetry of Gwendolyn Brooks*, unpublished dissertation (1966), p. 21.
10. Interview.
11. Garland, passim.
12. Clifton H. Johnson, editor, *God Struck Me Dead* (Philadelphia, 1969), pp. vii-xiii. Also helpful: Close reading of folk sermons.
13. Conversations.
14. Stavros, p. 15.
15. Lewis, p. 29.
16. Stavros, pp. 18-19.
17. Arthur P. Davis, "Gwendolyn Brooks: A Poet of the Unheroic," *CLA Journal*, 8 (December, 1963), p. 25.
18. Garland, pp. 49-52, & passim.
19. *Ibid.* (I saw a copy of the News Review,) courtesy of Miss Brooks.
20. The genesis of several poems is mention in Stavros, especially on pp. 7-8. I have also made deductions here and there.
21 Conversation with Miss Brooks.
22. Lewis, p. 28.
23. *Ibid.*

24. Conversation with Brooks & Don Lee.
25. Stavros, pp. 8, 12.
26. *We Asked Gwendolyn Brooks*, p. 4.
27. The quoted expressions are from the poem or Miss Brooks's paraphrase.
28. In Ida Lewis, p. 26.
29. Here and there among pp. 86-97.
30. Notes taken from the Proposal.

Baldwin
and the
Problem of Being

IN A *NEW YORK TIMES* BOOK REVIEW ESSAY, JAMES
Baldwin has stated that the effort to become a great novelist "involves attempting to tell as much of the truth as one can bear, and
then a little more."[1] It is likely in our time to mean attacking much
that Americans tend to hold sacred, in order that reality be confronted and constructively altered. As stated in "Everybody's Protest Novel," it means devotion to the "human being, his freedom
and fulfillment; freedom which cannot be legislated, fulfillment
which cannot be charted."[2] Baldwin then wishes to confront and
affect the human consciousness and conscience. He rejects the tradition of the protest novel because he feels that it denies life, "the
human being . . . his beauty, dread, power," and insists "that it is
categorization alone which is real and which cannot be trascended."[3]
He tries to write the way jazz musicians sound, to reflect their
compassion,[4] and it is noteworthy that Baldwin's tendency in *Go
Tell It On the Mountain* and *Another Country* is to focus upon the
individual characters' experiences in a way similar to Ralph Ellison's
description of Jazz:

> For true jazz is an art of individual assertion within and
> against the group. Each true jazz moment (as distinct from the
> uninspired commercial performance) springs from a contest in
> which each artist challenges all the rest; each solo flight or im-
> provisation, represents . . . a definition of his identity, as mem-
> ber of the collectively, and as a link in the chain of tradition.[5]

Reprinted from *CLA Journal, VII*, No. 3, March, 1964.

It should be generally observed that Baldwin's writings, owe much to Negro folk tradition (the blues, jazz, spirituals, and folk literature), and to the cihef experimental practioneers of modernist fiction, with especial emphasis upon Henry James.

The moral vision that emerges is one primarily concerned with man as he relates to good and evil and to society. For there is evil in human nature and evil abroad in the world to be confronted, not through Christianity whose doctrine tends to be the perverted tool of the ruling classes and groups whose bankruptcy was registered by the slaughter of the Jews during the Third Reich,[6] but through the love and involvement available from those able to eat of the tree of knowledge of good and evil and live. Within the breast of each individual, then, rages a universe of forces with which he must become acquainted, often through the help of an initiated person, in order to direct them for the positive growth of himself and others. The foregoing achievement is what Baldwin means by *identity*. To acjheve it, one must not be hindered by the detritus of society and one must learn to know detritus when one sees it.

Perhaps the question which throws most light upon Baldwin's work is simply: How can one achieve, amid the dislocations and disintegrations of the modern world, true, functional being? For Baldwin, the Western concept of reality, with its naive rationalism, its ignoring of unrational forces that abound within and without man, its reductivist activities wherein it ignores the uniqueness of the individual and sees reality in terms of its simplifications and categorizations is simply impoverishing. He who follows it fails to get into his awareness the richness and complexity of experience —he fails to be. And freedom is unattainable, since paradoxically, freedom is discovery and recognition of limitations, one's own and that of one's society;[7] to deny complexity is to paralyze the ability to get at such knowledge—it is to strangle freedom.

Groping unsteadily amidst the reductivist forces is an America which does not achieve, therefore, its primitive and essential moral identity. For the great vision that motivated the American adventure, there has been substituted a quest for spurious glory in mass production and consumption. And yet, ". . . there is so much more than Cadillacs, Frigidaires, and IBM machines. . . . One of the things wrong with this country is this notion that IBM machines *prove* something."[8] Still until America achieves its moral identity, its people, whether white or black, can fulfill nothing.

The struggle for identity, i.e., for functional being, is the major issue of Baldwin's first novel, *Go Tell It On the Mountain*. Attempting to tell part of the story found in the Negro's music, which "Americans are able to admire because a protective sentimentality limits their understanding of it,"[9] Baldwin examines three generations of a Negro family whose life span extends from slavery to the present day. The novel investigates, with warmth and perception, the Negro's possibility of achieving identity through the discipline of Christianity. The style is richly evocative, and one hears echoes of Joyce and Faulkner, the rhythms of the old time Negro sermon and the King James Bible. Unfolding in a series of major movements, the story proceeds as follows: the first movement introducing the reach of fourteen year old John Grimes for identity, a fearful, faltering reach, from a boy filled with guilt, hatred, fear, love, amidst the stern, religious frustrations of his elders and the pagan rebelliousness of his brother, Roy; the second presenting the tragedy of Florence, unable to overcome, among other things, the concept of the Negro she has internalized from the dominant culture—and therefore on insecure terms with herself and others; the third presenting Gabriel Grimes, stepfather of John, blocked from complete fulfillment by his attempts to escape his pagan drives in a fierce, frustrated embrace of Christianity; the fourth presenting Elizabeth, Mother of John, who after brief fulfillment in illicit love, retreats, frightened and awestricken, into the frustrated and frustrating arms of Gabriel Grimes. The final movement is the questionable flight of John Grimes from the quest for identity into the ostensible safety of religious ecstasy.

Vitally represented through a series of scenes occurring on his fourteenth birthday, reflected through images of poetic intensity, are the conflicts of young John. He stands upon a hill in New York's Central Park and feels "like a giant who might crumble this city with anger . . . like a tyrant who might crush this city with his heel . . . like a long awaited conqueror at whose feet flowers would be strewn, and before whom multitudes cried, Hosanna!"[10] Or concerning the rewards to be inherited from his preacher father: ". . . a house like his father's, a church like his father's and a job like his father's where he would grow old and black with hunger and toil. The way of the cross had given him a belly filled with wind and had bent his mother's back. . . ."[11] Mixed with his vision and perverting it is John's guilt over his sexual drives, the religious concept of the city as evil and the fatal tempter of the soul, and his parents' feeling that the city (New York) is filled with antagonistic whites who will block the worldly aspirations of Negroes. Over such obstacles John peers, enveloped in a solitude that seems well nigh unbreakable.

Part II, containing the stories of the adult members of the family who came to manhood and womanhood at the time of Emancipation, begins powerfully. Passionate scenes reveal the problems with which each character struggles. For Florence, the sister of the minister Gabriel, the central problem is to achieve an identity that excludes the concubinage already offered by her white Southern employer, the general sexual opportunism, or the image of the toil blasted bearer of children with its attendant heritage—a cabin like her mother's. In addition, Florence is one of a long line of Baldwin's characters who have absorbed from the dominant culture the concept of Blackness as low, contemptible, evil. Baldwin has said, "The American image of the Negro lives also in the Negro's heart; and when he has surrendered to this image life has no other possible reality."[12] Controlled by such an image, Florence flounders in a mixture of self-hatred, self-righteousness, sadism, and guilt feelings. Married to a ne'er-do-well, she succeeds merely in outraging herself and him, and in driving him away. She bows to religious ecstasy. Baldwin's point, of course, is that she was unable to achieve a life affirming love or her potential identity, and that her ecstatic surrender to Christianity as she nears the end of life is a gesture of desperation.

A man of titantic drives, Gabriel is a sufficient metaphor for man in a grim struggle with the forces of the universe; he stops just short of evoking the sense of tragedy, since self-recognition is not clerally confessed. What is available for articulating the self amid these forces, however, is a vision of St. Paul's Christianity which assures the self a Pyhrric victory by a repression that carries the mere coloring of a humanistic morality. Since sex, for Baldwin, is obviously a metaphor for the act of breaking one's isolation and, properly experienced, responsibly entering into the complexity of another human being, Gabriel's evasion of it by marrying the sexless Deborah (symbolically enough, mass raped by Southern whites and sterile) is his flight from dealing with his humanity. Baldwin contrasts him well with the pagan Esther, by whom a temporarily backsliding Gabriel begets a child he does not acknowedge. Esther has a firm concept of her dignity and humanity, and what is life-affirming and what is life-negating, and some of his fellow ministers, too, show that they do not take their fundamentalist concepts to rigid conclusions. Gabirel's response is to retreat more fiercely into religion, marry, after the death of Deborah the fallen Elizabeth, and harden in his grotesqueness.

Elizabeth is the ethical and moral center of the book. It is through her attachment to her father and reaction against her mother and aunt that she gains a sense of a love that is life giving. She knows that love's imprisonment is not a "bribe, a threat an indecent will to power"; it is "mysteriously, a freedom for the soul and spirit . . . water in dry places."[13] It seem to me, however, that Baldwin's hand falters in his analysis and presentation of her as a young woman. Her important relationship with her father, to the extent that it is at all rendered, is simply that of the conventional petting and "spoiling" afforded by a loose living man who does not take his fatherhood very seriously. That is to say that the father's free loving nature binds him to nothing, and, after cautioning Elizabeth (as we learn through a summary) never to let the world see her suffering, he returns to his job of running a house of prostitution. Amidst the religious illusions of the other characters, however, she retains a strong, quiet sense of her integrity, despite a relative commitment to religious passion.

Her fall came through her common-law husband, Richard, to whom she gave a self-sacrifical, life creating love. Although the portrayal of Richard as victimized by society and as a man whose being cannot fulfill its hunger is moving, the explanation of his curiosity and hunger seems oversimplified, if not, indeed, dehumanized: ". . . that I was going to get to know everything them white bastards knew . . . so could no white-son-of-bitch nowhere never talk me down, and never make feel like I was dirt. . . ."[14] Although the statement well reflects Richard's sensitivity and insecurity under the racial system of America, it hardly explains "his great adoration for things dead."

After the proud young Richard kills himself in reaction to extreme humiliation by the police who have imposed upon his consciousness the image of the low bestial Negro that he has tried to escape, Elizabeth gives birth to the bastard John, whose quest for identity forms the central movement of the book. As the second wife of Gabriel, she emerges as a person of complexity, and is sensitively involved in John's reach for life.

By a series of flashbacks, the author keeps us mindful that the present involves John Grimes's search for identity, the achievement of which is to be understood within the context of the lives of his elders. In the last section of the story, he is in crisis, and with the help of his friend Elisha, in a religious ecstasy, commits himself to the Cross. At various points, Baldwin uses a character by whose views the reality witnessed is to be qualified. In addition to the foreshadowings scattered throughout the story, there is Gabriel to point out that the ecstatic conversion is still to be tested by the long, complex journey of life. So quite without surprise, we encounter in a later short story. "The Death of the Prophet," an apostate Johnny who returns guiltily from some place of estrangement almost to collapse in the presence of his dying father.

That Baldwin in *Go Tell It on The Mountain* has drawn heavily upon autobiographical experiences is obvious, and those who like the pursuit can make interesting parallells with autobiographical situations reported in the essay collections: *Notes of a Native Son, Nobody Knows My Name,* and *The Fire Next Time.* But, from the artistic point of view, what is more interesting is their transmutation, their representation as organized energies that carry mythic force in their reflection of man attempting to deal with destiny. Much power derives from the confrontation of the ambiguity of life. That ambiguity carries into the various attitudes suggested toward the version of Christianity that his character relate themselves to. The relatively non-religious characters do not deny the relevance of God but seem to feel as Esther, the spurned mother of Gabriel's illegitimate child, puts it: ". . . that [the Lord's] spirit ain't got to work in everybody the same, seems to me."[15] Of the religiously engrossed characters, only Elizabeth achieves a relatively selfless being. However, the religion sustained the slave mother of Gabriel. Even for the twisted, it is a place of refuge, an articulation of the complexity of the mysterious forces of a demanding universe. But finally, the religious only partially illuminates, and the characters must grope in its light and bump against forces within and without that the religion has merely hidden or dammed.

With some admitted oversimplifications inescapable in tracing thematic lines, it may be said that in his two succeeding novels Baldwin is preoccupied with sex and love as instruments in the achievement of full being. As a novelist still under forty, he is no doubt creating works important to his total development, but in neither of these novels—*Giovanni's Room* and the best seller *Another Country*—does he seem to fully create his fictional worlds and characters; in short, he does not seem to have found characters who release his very real ability to create.

In an essay "Preservation of Innocence," Baldwin explicitly makes his criticism of popular concepts of sexuality. His chief point is that our rational classification of sexual characteristics and our efforts to preserve conventional norms tell us little about what it means to be a man or a woman. Our classifications are not definitive, and therefore we panic and set up safeguards that do nothing more than guard against sexual activities between members of the same sex. But such reductive simplicity, he argues, guarantees ignorance merely, or worse the probability that the bride and groom will not be able to add to the sum of love or know each other since they do not know themselves. Whatever position one takes regarding the argument, the following statements shed uncomfortable light upon the relationship between the sexes in much of American fiction:

> In the truly awesome attempt of the American to at once preserve his innocence and arrive at man's estate, that mindless monster, the tough guy, has been created and perfected, whose masculinity is found in the most infantile and elementary externals and whose attitude towards women is the wedding of the most abysmal romanticism and the most implacable distrust.[16]

Further complaint of the reductive approach to sexuality is contained in a review of Andre Gide's *Madeline*, in which he describes the possibility of communing with another sex as "the door to life and air and freedom from the tyranny of one's own personality. . . ."[17] And he describes our present day as one in which communion between the sexes "has become so sorely threatened that we depend more and more on the strident exploitation of externals, as, for example, the breasts of Hollywood glamor girls and the mindless grunting and swaggering of Hollywood he-men."[18] Despite our claim to knowledge, Baldwin implies, sex is a mystery that each person must find a way to live with.

In the light of the foregoing, it seems to me, Baldwin's intention in the novel *Giovanni's Room,* is more easily understood. The main line of the story portrays the way a youth's inherited definitions of sexuality fail him in his attempts to come to terms with his own, and adds to the sum of evil in his relationship with others. The chief character David represents the rational Westerner, who has absorbed the simplified, compartmentalized thinking of his background. Falling first in a romantic homosexual experience with a fellow adolescent Joey, he experiences that escape from isolation and the heightened spiritual awareness which love is supposed to bring. However, "A cavern opened in my mind, black, full of rumor, suggestion. . . . I could have cried, cried for shame and terror, cried for not understanding how this could have happened to me, how this could have happened in me."[19] Unresolved oedipal conflicts are hinted, and just when he needs spiritual sustenance from a father, his father, who knows nothing of the son's experience, insists upon retaining the simplified concept of himself as his son's "buddy." In flight from Joey, David repeats the mishap in the army, then takes flight to France to "find himself," but once there tentatively enters into a similar relationship with Giovanni. David expects Giovanni to be but an interval in life, since David has also a girlfriend Hella, a very rational minded girl who has gone to Spain to think out whether she is in love. But, moving just one step ahead of the predatory homosexual underworld, Giovanni's life demands David's love as its only hope for trascendence. Irresponsibly, and in a way that denies their complexity as human beings, David disappoints the hopes of Giovanni and disillusions Hella.

What Baldwin registers well is the desperate need for love that brings transcendence. The homosexual's problem is shown to be the threat of being forced into the underworld where bought love of the body, without transcendence, is simply productive of desperation. The women pictured face a similar problem on a heterosexual level. The world portrayed is nightmarish, but harldy, in any sense, really vital. One of its serious problems though is that the reader is

146

not allowed to escape the feeling, in the bad sense, of staginess and theatricality. The characters are in hell all right, but the reader never is, and I do not think that this is so simply because the approach to sex is unconventional. The characters do not root themselves deeply enough to become momentous in fictional terms, nor do they stand with intensity for elemental forces which we are forced to consider an inescapable part of our lives. So that, despite claims for complexity, the characters are too easily defined with relationship to a thesis.

Before coming to a consideration of *Another Country,* I should point out that Baldwin is the author of several stories of distinction, though there is hardly space for more than a brief mentioning of them. "Previous Condition" is the intense story of a young Negro's attempt to secure his being from its alienated condition within and the forces of prejudice without. It appeared in *Commentary,* October, 1948, as Baldwin's first story. "The Death of the Prophet," *Commentary,* March, 1950, was mentioned in connection with *Go Tell It on the Mountain."* "Come Out the Wilderness," *Mademioselle,* New York, 1961, explores the lostness of a Negro girl who has been alienated from her original racial environment. "Sonny's Blues," *Partisan Review,* Summer, 1957, reprinted in *Best Short Stories of 1958* and Herbert Gold's *Fiction of the Fifties,* New York, 1959, carries the venture of a Negro boy through narcotics to music where he finally gains a sense of identity expressed. "This Morning, This Evening, So Soon," *The Atlantic Monthly,* September 1960, reprinted in Martha Foley, *The Best Short Stories of 1961,* New York, 1961, an issue dedicated to Baldwin, explores the necessity of a successful young Negro actor to come to terms with his place in history. Each story shows a sure sense of the short story form, a moment of illumination that has significance for the total life of the character. Baldwin's greatest indebtedness in the short story is to Henry James.

Another Country, New York, 1962, Baldwin's latest novel, is a serious and ambitious attempt, a fact which should be recognized despite the fact that to make it a serious novel of the first rank would demand severe cutting and some intensive re-writing. The problem is still that of arriving at a definition of one's being, which will be adequately sustaining in the face of the evils of life, and to support another's complexity through love. Both heterosexual and homosexual scenes abound, but, as stated in the discussion of *Giovanni's Room,* these are the instruments for the exploration of being, the metaphors for self-definition and for responsibly entering the complexity of another. They have, therefore, a serious purpose, and Baldwin is too concerned about whether the sex experience provides a transcending love to make distinctions between the heterosexual and homosexual experience. Most of the men have engaged in a homosexual act, and have from it defined their sex for the future; that is, they decide whether the homosexual experience is or is not for their being, with most deciding in favor of heterosexuality.

The first story is that of Rufus, the Negro musician, who is fighting within himself both the real and the imaginary aspects of the race problem, and therefore cannot communicate with Leona, the Southern poor white girl that he picks up with the conscious purpose of sexual exploitation and of getting rid of her before she can "bug" him with her story (i.e., involve him in her complexity as a person). Rufus has suffered real racial persecution, so that even harmless remarks by Leona send him into a rage, and he finally drives her into a nervous breakdown and succumbs to his own frustrations by committing suicide. The horror of their experience is communicated with considerable skill. Rufus's failure in *being* is then re-tested in the lives of other characters who were, in varying degrees, associated with him.

Vivaldo Moore, the Irish-Italian, attracted to Rufus's sister, at first, partly through being a "liberal," and partly because of his sense of having failed her brother, must be made to confront her as a complex human conundrum, capable of ruthless exploitation and high level prostitution: that is, he must lose his innocence. Cass and Richard Silenski must abandon their oversimplified classification of each other and achieve a sense of reality in their marriage. Eric, the homosexual, must overthrow his Southern background and come to terms with himself in France. Everybody, indeed, must learn his own name. Thus the lives of successive sets of people must come against the problems of being, love and involvement.

One trouble with the scheme is that so few of the characters exemplify the complexity contended for them. Rufus, Ida, and Eric are the more adequately developed characters. The rest are not projected far enough beyond the level of nice, erring people. Thus the central problem of the book lacks momentousness. Ralph Ellison has said of the novel that ". . . it operates by amplifying and giving resonance to a specific complex of experience until, through the eloquence of its statement, that specific part of life speaks metaphorically for the whole."[20] It is precisely the foregoing illusion that *Another Country* in its totality is unable to create. The section concerned with the discovery of Rufus's death and the attendance at his funeral is excessive reportorial detail, sometimes theatrical, sometimes written at the level of the women's magazine. And the social criticism is inert, for the most part, a part of the chatty reflections of a particular character or of long clinical discussions.

On the other hand, there are some penetrating scenes that reflect the fine talent of Baldwin. In addition to the story of Rufus, I should cite most of the scenes where Ida is present and some of the scenes between Cass Silenski and Eric. In such scenes, the bold use of naturalistic devices—the sex scenes and four letter words—project meaning well beyond surface communication. What else could so well convey Rufus's horrified retching at his dilemma or the terrible exasperation of Ida and Vivaldo? Still, scenes abound in which naturalistic detail simply thickens the book and the four-letter words provide a spurious emphasis, galvanizing the reader's attention to no end. And yet *Another Country* is a book that has much to say, and, as I have tired to indicate, sometimes does.

It is not too much to assert then that Baldwin's novels since *Go Tell It on the Mountain,* though fine in segments, tend to reflect a hiatus in his artistic development. In *Go Tell It on the Mountain,* he was working with a body of understood, crystallized and only partially rejected religious and racial mythology that, therefore, carried coiled within it the wires of communication. It is not to say that the artist's challenge and task were simple to point out that he had primarily to manipulate the myth, to steep it in deliberate ambiguity, in order to reflect its Sphinx-like betrayal of those who uncritically absorbed it. The religious interpretation, after all, is within touching distance of the overall idea of Matthew Arnold's famous essay, "Herbraism and Hellenism." His autobiographical intimacy with such material required and received artistic skill and distance. Creating against such a background Baldwin effected a novel which transcended racial and religious categories—became an evoked image of man facing the mysterious universal forces.

On the other hand, the Baldwin of the last two novels confronts the modern consciousness amidst fluxions more talked about than crystallized, and moving at considerable speed: elements of modern man connoting fragmenting certainties eroded at the base, the succor for which has been sought mainly in the vague horizons of the backward look. The workings of sex amidst those fluxions are certainly, in the modern awareness, one major element in the choppy sea of our minds, in which definable shapes seem to appear for the purpose of disappearing. To define them artistically would seem to demand extraordinary effort indeed, whether in traditional or experimental terms.

The conclusion, therefore, to which a full reading of Baldwin seems inescapably to lead is that since his first novel he has not evolved the artistic form that will fully release and articulate his obviously complex awareness. And that to do so may require an abandonment of safety in the use of form equal to that which he has manifested in approach to subject, an act which may concomitantly involve estranging many of the multitude of readers which he has acquired. For an artist of Baldwin's fictional resources, talent, and courage, of his obvious knowledge of evolved fictional techniques, the challenge should hardly be overwhelming.

FOOTNOTES

1. James Baldwin, "As Much Truth As One Can Bear," *The New York Times Book Review* (January 14, 1962), p. 1.
2. *Notes of a Native Son* (Boston, 1955), p. 15.
3. *Ibid.*, p. 23.
4. 'What's the Reason Why: A Symposium by Best Selling Authors," *The New York Times Book Review* (December 2, 1962), p. 3.
5. Ralph Ellison, "The Charlie Christian Story," Saturday Review of *Literature* (May 17, 1958), p. 42
6. James Baldwin, *The Fire Next Time* (New York, 1063), p. 66.
7. "James Baldwin: An Interview," *WMFT Perspective* (December, 1961), p. 37.
8. *Ibid.*

9. *Notes of a Native Son*, p. 24.
10. *Go Tell It on the Mountain* (New York, 1953), p. 35.
11. *Ibid.*, p. 37.
12. *Notes*, p. 38.
13. *Go Tell It on the Mountain*, p. 210.
14. *Ibid.*, pp. 225-226.
15. *Go Tell It on the Mountain*, p. 161.
16. "Preservation of Innocence," *Zero* (Summer, 1949), pp. 18-19.
17. *Nobody Knows My Name* (New York, 1961), p. 161.
18. *Ibid.*, p. 162.
19. *Giovanni's Room* (New York, 1956), p. 12.
20. Granville Hicks, editor, *The Living Novel* (New York, 1957), p. 61.

Ralph Ellison
and
Afro-American Folk
and Cultural Tradition

RALPH ELLISON STRESSED CONNECTIONS BETWEEN Afro-American Folk and Cultural tradition and American culture, since "The heel bone is after all, connected, through its various linkages, to the head bone," and not to be ignored is "the intricate network of connections which binds Negroes to the larger society."[1] Mindful of this pronouncement I shall sketch in some of Ellison's ideas concerning the value of the folk tradition, explore representative techniques in *Invisible Man,* and offer suggested comments concerning the value and limitations of his method.

Pressed toward a bag of pure Blackness, Ellison was capable of minimizing folk tradition's value for the self-conscious writer, as he does in "Change the Joke and Slip the Yoke," an essay in response to Stanley Hyman's attempt to create archetypes of Blackness.[2] In "Change the Joke," he contended that the Black writer was "heir to the human experience which is literature," an inheritance which might be more important to him than his own living folk tradition. As for himself, Black folklore became important through literary discovery. Seeing the uses to which folklore is put in the works of James Joyce and T. S. Eliot, Ellison saw the folk tradition, the spirituals, blues, jazz and folk-tales as a stable factor in "the discontinuous, swiftly changing, and diverse American culture. . . ."[3] It expresses qualities needful in a world which exemplifies to a con-

Reprinted from *CLA Journal,* XIII, No. 3, March, 1970.

siderable degree a blues-like absurdity. It offers much to the writer, who can "translate its meaning into wider, more precise vocabularies."[4]

Actually, Ellison usually gave greater emphasis to folk traditions, and some allowance should be made for the fact that the primary goal of "Change the Joke" is to correct Stanley Edgar Hyman's concept of Black folklore. Since 1940, Ellison had been stressing its *ultimate* importance. In "Stormy Weather," a review of Langston Hughes's *The Big Sea,* which was critical of Hughes on other grounds, Ellison commended him for developing the national folk sources of his art.[5] Ellison's essay "Recent Negro Fiction" praised Hughes and Wright: Hughes for taking note of folklore and seeing the connection between his efforts and symbols and images of Negro forms; Wright, for attention to the Southern Negro folk.[6] In 1944, Ellison's short story, "Flying Home," made elaborate use of the Black folklore motif of the Black character who comes to grief in heaven for flying too imaginatively with his angel's wings. The main character, a Black aviator, finds peace only when he comes to terms with the survival values of folk tradition.[7]

In 1945, Ellison's essay entitled "Richard Wright's Blues,"[8] revealed a profound understanding of the *blues* as a folk cultural form and the value of its *forms* of response to existence for the self-conscious writer. He also analyzed the oppressive weight of American culture upon the folk, argued their complexity, and made a widely publicized definition of the *blues:*

> The blues is an impulse to keep the painful details and episodes of a brutal experience alive in one's aching consciousness, to finger its jagged grain, and to transcend it, not by the consolation of philosophy but by squeezing from it a near-tragic, near-comic, lyricism. As a form, the blues is an autobiographical chronicle of personal catastrophe expressed lyrically.[9]

Later in the same essay, he points out that the blues express "both the agony of life" and the possibility of overcoming it through sheer toughness of spirit. The blues are a valuable form also, in that they emphasize self-confrontation.

Comments upon the folk tradition are scattered among several essays in *Shadow and Act.* Perhaps the most emphatic occurs in

Ellison's responses during the 1955 Paris Interview.[10] He called attention to several functions of folklore and described some ways in which folklore worked dramatically in *Invisible Man*. Offering the first drawings of a group's character, preserving situations repeated in the history of the group, describing the boundaries of thought and feeling, projecting the group's wisdom in symbols expressing its will to survive, embodying those values by which it lives and dies, folklore seemed, as Ellison described it, basic to the portrayal of the essential spirit of Black people. In general, Ellison noted that great literature of France, Russia, and Spain was erected upon the humble base of folklore. Folk symbols serve Picasso as an annihilator of time through the use of simple lines and curves, and, for the viewer, a whole culture "may resound in a simple rhythm, an image." But most important, in its relationship to Black experience is Ellison's belief that the Black's folklore "announced the Negro's willingness to trust his own experience, his own sensibilities as to the definition of reality, rather than to allow his masters to define these crucial matters for him." Black American folklore, nonetheless, represents for Ellison an American and Western experience —"not lying at the bottom of it, but intertwined, diffused in its very texture."

Ellison also emphasizes the special qualities of a Black tradition in confronting reality, and describes them at some length in his essay, "The World and the Jug."[11] Suffice it here to say that they cover the gamut of attitudes for defining life positively, surviving oppression and extracting from existence many of its joys.

II

In *Invisible Man*, the whole gamut of Ellison's descriptions of the functions of folklore find their place. However, to be fully suggestive of their power is to bear in mind some specifics concerning the total reach of the novel. In the first place the novel's title is *Invisible Man*, not THE *Invisible Man*. In relationship to its nameless protagonist, the story delivers itself through at least three wavelengths, none in the form of the novel, completely separable from another: the hero as cosmic man, with the inescapable duty to gather up and affirm *Reality*, despite social oppression; the hero as victim, struggling with a cultural machinery that would reduce him to a negative sign; and the hero as an allegory of Black struggle in American history.

Black cultural and folk tradition frequently involves more than one of the wave-lengths.

In simplest form, we may see the interaction through several characters, who, in varying degrees, are folk or are a part of cultural tradition. In more complex form, the interaction of folk and cultural tradition ranges from motifs to situations, symbols, and strategic appearances of folk art forms: blues, spirituals, and folk rhymes.

The characters contrast with the lostness of the invisible narrator, since they represent Reality confronted. Thus the slave woman envisioned singing spirituals in the prologue is used to comment upon the pain of victimization, but she and her sons also define *freedom,* a basic theme of the novel, as the ability to articulate the self, and as a question that can be answered only by each individual's confrontation with the self. Louis Armstrong and his jazz reflect both an articulated self and a mode of breaking through the ordinary categories of Western clock time. The grandfather who appears at strategic points throughout the novel is a reflector of bitter past and continuing victimization. On the other hand, he is, in Ellison's words, the "ambiguity of the past," a sphinx-like riddle which must be approached creatively and not in the literal minded fashion which actually makes of the invisible narrator an accessory to the Brotherhood's crime of provoking a riot in Harlem. Yet the destruction of whites by yessing and confirming their false sense of reality, which the invisible narrator has imitated with nearly fatal consequences, was a solid survival technique of his grandfather and the folk.

Trueblood and Mary, who have assimilated both folk and general Black cultural tradition, play the most powerful dramatic roles among the folk figures. Trueblood, with whom the invisible narrator inadvertently confronts philanthroper Norton, is several roles. On the simple folk level, he is a person who can face the results of his humanity: becoming an expectant father by both his wife and his daughter.

He achieves a conclusion, which the brainwashed and pragmatic invisible narrator requires most of the novel to grasp: "I ain't nobody but myself." His achievement is dramatized through the rituals of first singing spirituals—and then the blues. Singing the spirituals dramatizes his struggle and pain. But it is the singing of the blues, the folk form which Ellison has celebrated for its ritual of self-confrontation, that enables Trueblood to get himself together. In Chapter Nine, the blues *forms of response* to existence becoming meaningful to the invisible narrator as a street singer celebrates the *absurdity* of a self committed passionately to a woman with "feet like a monkey" and "legs like a frog," and the narrator, realizing how Bledsoe has duped him, can laugh bitterly at himself by singing, "they picked poor robin clean." But it is Trueblood who exemplifies the real toughness of the tradition, and also the racy humor, the folk story-telling tradition, the highly flavored speech, and the capacity for enjoyment of life.

But Trueblood is also interconnected with American and Western tradition. He is, on one hand, the testimony to the density of reality that Western rationalism evades. And he is, on the other, American and Western scapegoat, frankly admitting the sins of the flesh, the full acknowledgment of which the philanthroper Norton dodges by Platonic and puritanical sublimation. For Norton too has committed incest with his daughter but mentally, rather than physically. And the white Southern community acknowledges its secret sexual longings and Trueblood's role as their substitute bearer of sin by dropping coins into his pocket.

But more broadly still, Trueblood connects finally with Western incest tradition and with Freud.[12] Like Oedipus he has invaded unaware the zone of taboo. For he cohabited with his daughter while dreaming. So, was he guilty? Selma Fraiberg argues persuasively that in Freudian terms he was, since he was the author of the dream which his being conjured up for the purpose of allowing the sexual act. At any rate, Trueblood must bear up while the gods deliberate indefinitely concerning the sins of mortal man.

It will be remembered that Mary Rambo is the Southern migrant —now New York mistress of a boarding house—into whose hands the invisible narrator falls after barely surviving the allegorically represented attempt of the industrial system to eliminate all potential for individuality and reduce him to anonymity. The elaborate role that Ellison had designed for Mary may be examined in the fragment published in Herbert Hill's anthology of contemporary Black literature, *Soon One Morning*.[13] Mary is the warmth, wit, coping power, and humanity of the folk tradition as it survives in the modern industrial city. And she is the integration of the bitter past with the present, as can be seen by her possession of such purely survival items as the bank topped by a minstrel figure, "a very black, red lipped and wide mouth Negro, his face an enormous grin, his single large black hand held palm up before his chest." In Chapter Fifteen, where he appears, the invisible narrator tries unsuccessfully to drop the symbols of the past, which must be integrated into his being. Unlike Trueblood, Mary is not merged with Western symbols independent of her, a fact of dramatic significance since the hero's recovery from the industrial onslaught is managed through complete, though temporary, retreat into Blackness. Also, unlike Trueblood, Mary makes a strong positive impact upon the invisible narrator, although he must symbolically leave her and become powerless to return as he mounts higher into the abstractions of rationalism through the Brotherhood and as he retreats into the freely imaginative self.

Another folk figure is Dupre, the leader of Harlem rioters who burn down a tenement building. The dramatic and symbolic function of Dupre and his followers is to reflect the folk ability to move with poise amidst chaos and in contradiction to the flat rational assumptions of the Brotherhood concerning its mission as planners for others. The rioters move with a plan that directly confronts Reality.

The discussion of the foregoing characters illustrates, rather than exhausts, the role of folk or folkish characters. We must turn now to scenes that are informed with folk motifs. Ellison himself has commented upon the early Battle Royal scene as one that he lifted from living rituals and placed in a context of larger meaning.[14] It and the invisible narrator's speech comprise on one wave length the ultimate in oppression and self-victimization, as the invisible protagonist tries to be pragmatic and economic man. In the highest sense of the word, the scene is both horrible and wildly comic.

It involves several motifs from folk tradition, a full explanation of which would comprise a separate essay. On the level of Blackness, there is the manipulation of Blacks to fight each other blindly, education as brainwash, the general white manipulation of reality, and the shaping of misleaders of the people. The narrator, himself, embodies the sardonic folk concept that "what's white is right."

157

But one of the powerful folk motifs is the racial joke of black man and tabooed white woman. The unwritten folk joke, from which the scene derives, is concerned with a Black looking at a white woman and expressing sexual desire while a white man stands by and replies.

Black. Oh man, will I ever, ever!
White. No Nigger, you will never, never!
Black. As long as there's life there's hope!
White. Yeah Nigger, and as long as there's trees there's rope.

In the Battle Royal scene, it will be recalled, the Black boys are forced to watch the nude white woman dance, and are abused if they look and abused if they do not look. In terms of Blackness, the ritual is to stamp upon them the symbolic castration they are supposed to experience in the presence of a white woman.

Ellison, however, makes his connections. He dramatizes the perverted responses of the white men, and the American flag tattooed upon the nude woman's belly as satire upon American corruption of sexuality. He unites the invisible narrator and the nude blonde as victims and makes out of her a symbol implying the mystery of freedom, similar to James Joyce's use of woman in *A Portrait of the Artist as a Young Man:* "She seemed like a fair bird-girl girdled in veils calling to me from the angry surface of some gray and threatening sea."[15]

Perhaps enough attention has been given to the unconstrained density of reality represented by people, folk and non-folk, of the Golden Day, the sporting house where the philanthroper Norton is faced with all the reality that his rational categories have suppressed. I focus instead upon the vesper scene in Chapter Five, a poem really, in which folk, Black cultural tradition in general and Western mythology merge. Ellison, in this chapter, is not without humor, but he extracts, at times tenderly, a deep pathos for the uplife dreams that somehow ought to be true. The narrator looks upon them as his investment in identity. The folk motif is the remembered coming of a Moses to bring freedom and richness to the barren land, a ritual and myth delivered in the rich rhetoric of the Black speech tradition. Of course, Homer Barbee, the priest who summons up pictures of ancestors to validate the myth is blind—a device for undermining his credibility.

Ellison combines the Black Moses myth with the Biblical Moses and the rituals traditionally describing the miraculous birth and survival of the hero. For good measure, the students are also involved in the rites of Horatio Alger. The combination carries the chapter to one of the memorable intensities of the novel. And adding still more to the pathos is the ex-slave matron, Susie Greshman, who brings the warmth and tragic knowledge of the folk—and their high hopes to this colorful but ineffectual ritual. Anyone who has sat through ceremonies that achieve such a high sense of group communion and shared memories will identify briefly with the invisible narrator despite his terrible delusion.

Such folkish scenes appear also at strategic points in the section of the book devoted to the narrator's Northern experiences, and Ellison exacts from them, at will, humor, pathos, and philosophy. The hero's transition to the impersonal Northern experience evokes memories of folklore deriving from the Southern Black's initiation into Northern urban life. The black man-white woman motif arises in a comic scene where the crush of subway traffic jams the narrator against a white woman: "I wanted desperately to raise my hands, to show her it was against my will." I have already referred to the pivotal confrontation with Mary, symbol of all that is positive and something of the negative in folk tradition.

I shall mention briefly additional scenes—all of which function mainly in the exemplification of Blackness. In Chapter Eleven, the highly symbolic section which portrays the tendency of industrialism to reduce men to a programmed zero, the Brer Rabbit motif emphasizes the toughness of the Black experience, the indestructibility of a fiber, which is later restored through the care of the folkish Mary Rambo. The numerous folk symbols appearing in different scenes within Chapter Thirteen range in significance from the hero's *elementary* awakening to his heritage through the evoking of the entire Black tradition in the eviction of the ex-slave couple, Mr. and Mrs. Primus Provo, a couple who also embody the bitter fruits harvested by Blacks since securing freedom.

The self-contained and bitter pride of the Provoses has an affinity with the feelings evoked in Chapter Thirteen by Brother Tarp, a man who spent nineteen years on the chain gang for opposing white imposition before escaping to New York. Tarp passes on to the invisible narrator a link from the chain broken to secure his freedom. Symbolically, it is a bitter link in the chain of Black tradition, meant to serve as a reminder of roots and inescapable contours in the profile of Black reality. Other images of Blackness appear as warnings as the invisible narrator moves deeper into the Brotherhood: the minstrel fascism of the Brother Wrestrum, who provokes the Brotherhood trial of the narrator; the minstrel dolls manipulated ritualistically to express the youth organizer Todd Clifton's deep sense of betrayal, and the allied image of the zoot-suited Black boys playing their bitter hip satire upon "history" in Chapter Twenty; and perhaps we may include Ras the Exhorter whose existence and strength (Todd Clifton: ". . . it's on the inside that Ras is strong . . . dangerous.") are based first upon the urban folk's hunger for identity and nationhood and second, at least latently, in the breast of every Black conscious of loss and of deep and sustained betrayal. With Rinehart, symbol of possibility through imagination and masking, we are back to Western tradition.

However, Ellison has a deep sense of the beauty, as well as the terror of Black tradition, and therefore acknowledgment of his rendering the rich folk language of the South, the salty speech of the Northern urban areas, and the joyful myth making of urban narrators in the Harlem riot scene is probably the proper note on which to draw toward conclusions.

The first conclusion is that, along with other devices, the folk tradition affords the Black writer a device for instant movement into the privacy, tensioned coherence, toughness, terror and beauty of Black experience—a method for conjuring up instant Blackness. It is to be noted that Ellison tends to use folk tradition without making outside connections in some scenes emphasizing the height of betrayal of Blackness (as in the Primus Provo eviction), in those portraying dramatic recoil of the narrator from illusions, or in those especially emphasizing a reverential treatment of folk value. But the principle is not fixed: the over-riding guide is utility to theme and dramatic structure. The vesper scene at the Southern college, it will be recalled, derives from Black folklore and Western mythology.

Folklore does not appear then at any point for its own sake, nor is folk vision sentimentalized. As reverently as the folk Mary Rambo is treated, she is not seen as useful to the highest abstract reaches of personality. This view is in line, by extension, with Ellison's concept of Southern folk community as a pre-individual community.[16] So it is not surprising that, once having absorbed what he can from her and having reached for more abstract levels of personality, the invisible narrator cannot return. Another example of the non-sentimental approach is the invisible narrator's newly gained appreciation of soul food, a passage which has been widely quoted for its humor and evidence of acceptance of identity. But the narrator realizes that identity on this level is really too simple. Further, as he continues to eat yams, one turns out to be frost-bitten—not mere sweetness.

Yet there is something of the great performance, the *tour de force*, in Ellison's use of the folklore and cultural tradition that makes for both enlightenment regarding the literary potential of folklore and a certain unease. This response, I think, is inspired by the elaborate system of interconnection with Western symbols and mythology, and our awareness that Blackness is more in need of definition than Western tradition, which has had the attention of innumerable literary masters. It has to do with the degree of faith that one has in the West, and the suspicion that major literary documents from Melville through Faulkner have been whispering to us of its death. And, in the Black tradition, there has been so frequently an ambivalence and a questioning of the West that go deeper than casting a critical eye upon its technology and rationalism.

The question raised by Larry Neal regarding Ellison's relationship to the West in his critical essays may well be raised regarding the interconnection system in *Invisible Man*, since there is almost a mathematical consistency between Ellison's critical pronouncements and his creative performance. Writing in *Black Theatre*, Neal credited Ellison with a broad theoretical sense of Black folklore tradition and culture, and an awareness of the "explosive tensions underlying the Black man's presence in the United States," but criticized him for overlaying "his knowledge of Black culture with concepts that exist outside it."[17]

Certainly, the result in *Invisible Man*, if one commits himself to a grasp of the depths of the book, is sometimes simultaneously an awe at sheer brilliance of conjunctions and a hunger for further depths of definition of Blackness which this wily genius obviously has the capacity to make. For make no mistake about it, anyone who could throw in those images of Blackness with such rapidity and apparent ease, who could tone their depths as a gifted musician would do, has, as a pressure behind his imagination, an almost god-like knowledge of Blackness. Make no mistake, Ellison paid his dues to culture. At no time does one run into Blackness that is rhetorical only, as one still frequently does in even very radical writing. But Ellison, himself, admits that the book would have been better if it had had more of Mary Rambo.[18] We would add to Mary, more of Bledsoe, more of the campus dreamers, more of the Harlem rioters, and more even of B. P. Rinehart and Ras, the Destroyer. And we would suppose that it is possible to sound the depths of the universe by a fine excess in the examination of Blackness. A William Faulkner, for example, in making us feel the American and Western aspect of his universe, simply asserts himself as the deepest of Southerners, and communicates through symbols most deeply associated with the South. Perahps the Faulknerian way is one for the future, since neither the spirit of the 1950's nor the temperament and sensibility which Ellison has frequently and emphatically expounded suggest that earlier, in dealing with Blackness, a Black focus would have been successful or that it would have found an audience.

In the end, it is the great fruits at hand which Ellison harvested that must be seized upon. For the young writer, his use of folk tradition provides a veritable textbook which can be adapted, according to one's own sensibility and outlook. For more than any other writer, Ellison grappled with its power, its cryptic messages, its complexity. Particularly noteworthy is his realization that folk tradition cannot seem, in a self-conscious artist, to be an end in itself. That is, the writer cannot simply enclose himself within the womb of folkness or content himself with simple celebration of folkness. True folk forms have already celebrated folk life better than the self-conscious artist can hope to do. But the basic *attitudes* and *forms* of response to existence evolved by the folk are abandoned by us only at our peril. These attitudes and forms of response are then of greatest service as flexible instruments for confronting a darkness that is always changing in its complexity. Ellison exemplified a profound knowledge of all such ramifications.

FOOTNOTES

1. Ralph Ellison, *Shadow and Act* (New York, 1964), p. 253.
2. Both authors' essays first appeared in *Partisan Review* (Spring, 1958). Ellison's essay is reprinted in *Shadow and Act*, Hyman's in *The Promise End* (New York, 1963).
3. *Shadow and Act*, p. 58.
4. *Ibid.*, p. 59.
5. *New Masses*, 37 (September 24, 1940), 20-21-
6. *New Masses*, 40 (August 5, 1941), 22-26.
7. James A. Emanuel and Theodore L. Gross, *Dark Symphony* (New York, 1968), pp. 254-270.
8. *Shadow and Act*, pp. 77-94.
9. *Ibid.*, p. 78 f.
10. *Ibid.*, pp. 167-186. The entire interview merits careful study.
11. *Shadow and Act*, here and there, pp. 107-143.
12. See Selma Fraiberg, "Two Modern Incest Heroes," *Partisan Review*, XXVIII (1961), pp. 646-661. In this section, I am very much indebted to her essay.
13. Herbert Hill, *Soon One Morning* (New York, 1963).
14. *Shadow and Act*, p. 174.
15. *Invisible Man*, p. 23.
16. *Shadow and Act*, p. 90.
17. Larry Neal, "Cultural Nationalism and Black Theatre," *Black Theatre*, No. 1, p. 10.
18. See unused section of hospital scene, Herbert Hill, *Soon One Morning* (New York, 1963).

Faulkner and the Heritage of White Racial Consciousness: Notes on White Nationalism in Literature

FRANTZ FANON, IN *BLACK SKINS WHITE MASKS, SPEAKS* of the weight upon black minds cast by the white collective unconscious which is culturally transmitted from generation to generation. This white unconsciousness defined "is purely and simply the sum of prejudices, myths, and collective attitudes of a given group."[1] By a process which Fanon calls "cultural imposition" the collective attitudes, prejudices and myths, are hurled powerfully and often subtly from the cultural instruments and institutions of the dominant white groups and tend to cripple and enslave the minds of Blacks. In America, W. E. B. DuBois had much earlier taken note of the impact of cultural imposition upon the minds of Blacks and had seen it as the producer of a destructive warfare in conscious, which he described in *The Souls of Black Folks*.[2]

As slaves and as quasi-free men, Blacks have effected physical survival by cultivating a sensitive and super-alert awareness of the threatening impulses of the white consciousness. Black folklore celebrates this super-alert response in a joke regarding impending racial violence: "Nigger, read and run. If you can't read, run!" In our cultural revolution, however, the objective is not mere survival or physical security—but complete psychological freedom, a fact which demands that we neutralize any blood sucking tentacles of the white consciousness and thus empower ourselves to release the full force of our creative power and critical judgment.

Literature is one instrument by which a dominant class or race asserts its interests, preserves its heritage and values, and preempts for them the category of the universal. Reinhold Niebuhr, in *Moral Man and Immoral Society,* long ago noted the tendency of privileged groups and classes to make unconscious and conscious identification of their special interests with general interests and universal values, especially when they cannot be rationally defended. As V. F. Calverton pointed out in "Art and Social Change," a literary critic functions within a class or group objective, and not in terms of an absolute, although he may think that he is functioning "freely." He makes his judgments in the terms of his culture and in reference to his personal and "immediate heritage." Thus V. F. Calverton sees artists, intellectuals, critics and others as operating, inescapably, within a *cultural compulsive.* Defined: "The Cultural compulsive represents the group interest in its psychological form." Thus a critic's ability to bring an author to the forefront is less dependent upon doctrinal truth or *universalism* than upon his adaptability to the class or group interest which he subserves.

In the light of the above, the black critic of white literature, must not, as white critics can do and remain in harmony with their group's interest, confront a white work by hustling with jet speed to the "universal." If he does, he may fail to note that the bag he is poking his head into is chock full of special cultural interests. Regarding Faulkner, he will not be put off by a critic like Cleanth Brooks saying that Faulkner's *Sound and the Fury* is not so much about the *South* (the book's particularism) as it is about the *family* (a move to universalism).[4] Nor will he be completely sold by those who helped to establish Faulkner's position at the forefront of contemporary writers by emphasizing that Faulkner's work is about *Man.* He will want to run his fingers very carefully over all the lineaments, the tensioned particulars, specific toning of racial incidents and characters, the particular hang-ups of the white characters, and the peculiar conditions under which the reader has to grasp the existence of black characters in Faulkner's fiction. He may then, at some time in the wee dawn hours, risk some statement about the universals. In other words, he will not be blinded by the fact that Faulkner's preoccupations happen to coincide with those of the white liberal critical establishment.

The special cultural compulsives of Western culture, its economic motives, and exploitation of the image of the stranger, are touchstones, with which to identify the *symbolic needs* of the white consciousness and to understand its condition. The following is an illustrative list of cultural drives on which America as a Western exaggeration, has attempted to place a pre-empting signature:

1. Endorsement of intense individualism and extreme self-consciousness, often leading to alienation.
2. Drive to mastery over Nature—often creating uneasiness regarding relationship to nature.
3. Pre-emption of the doctrine of evolution and progress for evidence of Western status as a natural outcome.
4. The drive for massive and intricate organization.
5. Possession of Christianity as a status-endowing religion and a validation of the role of Western white men (negative ordering of the flesh—*Light in August*).
6. Versions of rationality and common sense as efficient tools for dealing with reality.
7. Possession of a problem-solving optimism.
8. Economic self-interest and concentrated exploitation.

When confronting Blackness, white writers are free to take a variety of attitudes toward the listed cultural drives, but they can not escape the fact that, as much as skin color, the cultural drives are transmitted by cultural instruments as the definition of whiteness. Lasting literature derives from our deepest consciousness, and the evidence from literature is that even alienated white writers can not push aside these cultural drives sufficiently to come into the court of racial imagination with "clean" minds. They create a mythicization of the designated stranger and Blackness, a proliferation of racial myth and ritual, and a use of the designated stranger and Blackness for the validation of whiteness. Our evidence is the frequency and intensity with which certain images of Blackness are hungrily insisted upon, which notify us that we are being offered grains of reality upon a ground of myth.

A twisted relationship to the above cultural drives creates the white character as literal outcast or spiritual outcast who as outcast cannot return to white society. As Leslie Fielder long ago pointed out.[5] The white as an outcast then seeks the love of a colored man

—a nature symbol. As I have said, although he seems to frequently receive, in this state, both catharisis and conversion he cannot return to the white racist society and figures of Blacks are fantasies of symbolic and psychic needs—in a word his sickness.

Huck Finn can only light out for the territory.

Faulkner's Isaac McCaslin, for many white critics Faulkner's moral center, grabs the heart of the Negro-Indian, Sam Fathers, in the first three parts of "The Bear." But in the difficult 4th part where he re-enters society, for all the emotionalizing over Sam Fathers, Isaac returns to his tribal heritage. The last major role we see him performing in "Delta Autumn," he is screaming all kinds of racist stuff.

A certain amount of sickness in Faulkner's fiction results from Faulkner's attempt to bring the spiritual outcast to terms with his society, and resolution of the problem is apparent only, while sickness roils in the fabric of the plot: Chick Mallison and Gavin Stevens in Faulkner's *Intruder in the Dusk,* Miss Habersham in "Go Down Moses," Carothers Edmonds in the "Fire and the Hearth" and the cheap theatrics of the black Ringo and the white Bayard Sartoris in *The Unvanquished.*

From such sickness, we get our images of Blackness in white literature.

The reality principle only partly shapes their contours: the fretful, feminized black male servants, the images of black women as raw natural sex or as myths of eternal love in a timeless Eden, have more questionable sources—the symbolic needs of a sick white consciousness.

In passing, it may thus be noted that if Faulkner overcame aspects of Southern white consciousness, he was still a part of the general American white consciousness and its symbolic needs. The South simply exemplified more concretely the economic and psychological rituals that arise in the confrontation of the white consciousness with Blackness. In sensing Faulkner's heritage, it will be useful to take some note of the white consciousness in Europe, to see its operation in America, and then to comment upon Faulkner's own rendering of selected situations.

In relationship to Europe, I find useful G. K. Hunter's essay in *Shakesperean Survey,* entitled "Elizabetheans and Foreigners."[6] Hunter states that the impact of foreigners on a community or a

167

culture is shaped "by the opportunities for contact and knowledge that exists, and by the framework of cultural assumptions within which information about foreign lands and customs is presented and received." In other words—their cultural compulsives. The weight of Hunter's essay will illustrate the importance of Christianity as a major strand in the network of what I have called the white cultural compulsive. Regarding religion, indeed, V. F. Calverton acknowledges its major role prior to the impact of the doctrine of evolution: "If before 1859, Western civilization found its intellectual continuity in biblical doctrine, after 1859, it found its new continuity in the doctrine of evolution."[7]

Hunter's cultural analysis is as follows.[8] He describes the Middle Ages as a period during which physical geography had no real meaning in itself. What counted was spiritual geography. Regarding other nations, the Westerner was concerned with their spiritual distance from the Holy Land, ". . . the natural hub of Christian experience. . . ." Those on the "fringe of the circumambient waters —pagans, Leviathan (both the whale and the Devil), together with Negroes, apes, semi-homines and others" comprised a group "whose distance from full humanity could be measured by their geographical distance from that area where humanity had been most fully realized in the life of Christ." The Ptolemaic "three-fold world," Hunter continues, conceived of Africa as inhabited by the descendants of Ham, Asia by those of Shem, and Europe by those of Japhet. As physical places, neither Africa nor Europe had meaning: The Middle Ages had settled their "theological statuses," and that was enough. Obviously, one role of Christianity was to give free elbow room for mythicization of the stranger. *The Travels of Sir John Mandeville,* a fantastic work that spoke of headless persons whose eyes were in their shoulders and mouths in the middle of their breasts, was the most popular of the European travel books up to the middle of the Eighteenth Century.

Hunter explains that, since European nations largely shared the same theological assumptions down through the Renaissance, they did not appear to each other as separate and contrasting images. Something could be made of various national groups to express the idea of hot blood or of "absurd deviations from the English norm." The Elizabethan author, therefore, went beyond Europe and drew upon ancient oppositions—the conflict between God and the Devil, between Christian and anti-Christian. Such oppositions were represented by the Jew, the Turk, and the Moor..

With the Moor, we come closer to the mythic responses that hemmed in the Blacks of Faulkner, the South, and America. The Moor was considered foolish or wicked prior to the appearance of Othello, an exception to the considerable confusion that seemed to exist as to whether the Moor was a human being or a monster. Othello is apparently an "inversion of expected racial values." But he is seen variously as "the thick lips," "the Devil with collied complexion"—in short, Hunter concludes, as a "coal-black Negro." In general, the Moors represented the opposite values to those of the "European norm of civilized white Christian," and offered special advantage "for the presentation of *a priori wickedness*." For "however large was the 'bottle nose'" that Henslowe used to present the Jew on the stage, it could not have had "the impact of the total sable of the Moor; "which was seen as the emblem of Hell, of damnation, as the natural livery of the Devil." The Devil frequenty appeared to Europeans, in their religious fantasies, in the body of a Moor. Hunter quotes the 18th Century writer Samuel Butler in summation of the responses:

> Some with the devil himself in league grow
> By's representative, a Negro.

In regard to "Othello," I might add, despite his status as an "inversion of expected racial values," he remains a mythicized Black, an example of the inability of the author to escape entirely from his cultural compulsives. If Othello as expected devil, turns out to be, instead, a salvaged, martial angel, he is also a narcissistic tribute to the nobility of the White European Venetian State, whose shining light has guided him away from savagery. In today's terms, he has been programmed. For it is Othello's upward slanted eyes in fierce admiration of the State and his sacred worship of its white female that have put into order his savage energies and allowed his nobility to emerge. And the audience's assumptions, in a sense, are not proved entirely wrong. The fool exists also—and the wicked; the barbarian strangles the pure white Venetian lady. We may well keep in mind this "inversion of expected racial values" for the encounter with Faulkner's major black figures, Dilsey and Lucas Beauchamp.

The situation worsens, as we return to America, in its direct racial impact upon multitudes of white people. The transplanted Europeans whose energy enabled the ruthless re-settlement of a continent, were both less constricted and less secure psychologically in the confrontation with Blackness. Within the European state, the majority experienced the confrontation with Blackness primarily on a theoretical and abstract level. While they reaped the profits and crumbled the unity of Man, Europeans, in their own country, could conceive of the "native" as something vague in a distant land, not sullen Blackness in the plantation cabin or across the wagon trail. Myth and ritual, under such circumstances, easily perform their duties: the warding off of chaos and the shaping of reality into comfortable patterns. Romantic myth and ritual do their thing, and we hear of "the white man's burden," the "Christianizing of the heathen," the bringing of "civilization to the hordes without the law." Assumptions concerning the humanistic content of European culture could be protected without producing, locally, torrid and intense emotional conflicts.

However, in America masses of transplanted Europeans directly confronted the presence of Indians—and soon, the presence of Blacks, Europeans, in flight from constraining institutions, soon confronted both Inidans and Blackness through rawer and cruder forms and fell directly into rapid and intensely wielded gestures. The Indians occupied needed lands, the answer was robbery and genocide. The land required labor for the rapid accumulation of wealth, and the answer was the enslavement of the mind and body of the Black slave. Along the way, racial myths and rituals abounded. Even after the Civil War, the most distinguished and revered educational institutions blandly busied themselves in the institutionalization of racism, in the name of learned theories and "scientific" developments. Thomas Y. Gossett in *Race, the History of an Idea in America,* has given, in scholarly detail, the growth of the institutionalism of racism and the participation of most learned disciplines.[9] During periods of white insecurity the racism is crude, but becomes refined, during periods of security, bereft of the stiffness and obvious brutality that were produced during economic and other stressful conflicts. The Indian is no longer in receipt of the status that the "only good in'jun is a dead in'jun," he is, instead, a harmless television joke. The physical chains are separated from the Blacks, who are no longer benighted Blacks of Manichean propensities, but the culturally disadvantaged. From a variety of institutions, they receive a highly polished brainwashing and learn to mirror themselves through the eyes of the oppressor. They receive, that is, an "education."

II

Such then is Faulkner's general heritage of white racial consciousness. What of the purely literary heritage? If we consider major American writers, the answer is short: Nil. Although Mark Twain slightly stirred himself in the enshrined adventure of Huck Finn and Nigger Jim, and Herman Melville used exotics and other nature symbols in his quarrels with 19th Century Society, the best that we can say is that we are alerted to certain things involving the white consciousness: that its narcissism is overgrown and at times obscene; that any intense relationship between a white character and a black is likely to be symbolically a relationship between the white character and nature; and that the black character must always be related to the state of weather in the white consciousness.

As to the specific white consciousness of Faulkner, we can now begin with the common outlook that infested his region and range toward his identification with the contemporary liberalism that established him. We can comment upon certain strategic works and such characters as Isaac McCaslin of "The Bear," and end by comments upon black characters.

Faulkner's consciousness focused upon the Southern past. He was of a generation of Southern writers, who were trying to get all those Southern ghosts of the past off their backs. Snatching them around so that he could trace their images, he could say nasty things, occasionally, about them as he struggled to free himself to grasp a sound reality principle. But Faulkner was looking for something called "wholeness." And he found it in the mythic past. Through the voice of Jason Compson, Sr., in *Absalom, Absalom!* Faulkner announces the value of the white figures of the pre-Civil-War South:

> ... People too as we are, and victims too as we are, but victims of different circumstances, simpler and therefore, more heroic, too, not dwarfed and involved but distinct, uncomplex who had the gift of loving once or dying once instead of being diffused

171

and scattered creatures drawn blindly limb from limb from a grab bag and assembled. . . .[10]

To gather up the Southern past, Faulkner told the writer Robert Cantwell that he did not read history. He saturated himself by talking to Southern white people, who had lived through the Civil War. He and other boys would play Civil War games, and the old men "would tell us what it was like.[9] One, of course, recalls the numerous legends and myths that once passed for Southern "history." If one does not, some of them are available enough in printed form in the *Publications of the Mississippi Historical Society* of the turn of the Century.[11] The sources are often the memories of veterans and "prominent citizens" concerning such issues as the overthrowal of Reconstruction in various Mississippi Counties. Complex issues become simply a struggle between the Anglo-Saxon sons of Light and the Manichean forces of Chaos and the Void. A Miss Julia Kendal wrote the history of Reconstruction in Faulkner's Lafayette County—a lurid story in which the black sons of darkness and the Northern fallen sons of Light do deeds that make angels weep. Eventually, the long-suffering rage of virtuous white Anglo-Saxon manhood breaks loose, and the heads of Blacks bob in the Mississippi Yocana River.

A somewhat frightening reflection of the hangups of Faulkner's local sources. But let's don't knock it. First, Faulkner was really a widely read man, who was simply given to the anti-intellectual stance common to American writers. Second, the provincial historians, from the point of view of whites, did give him a chance to grasp the inner realities of legends as they operated in the white consciousness. The whole affair, of course, leaves him up against a test: depth of understanding and perception, breadth of vision, and functional detachment. Guilt, fear, and self-justification, are the more searing conflicts of the white consciousness, requiring the exorcism of myth and rite and the massaging of symbolic needs. W. J. Cash, in *The Mind of the South,* draws attention to their operation:

Mrs. Stowe (author of *Uncle Tom's Cabin*) did not invent the figure of Uncle Tom, nor did Christy invent that of Jim Crow —the banjo-picking heel-flinging, hi-yi-ing happy jack of the levees and the cotton fields. All they did was to modify them a little for their purposes. In essentials both were creations of the South—defense mechanisms, answers to the Yankee and its own doubts, projections from its own mawkish laughter over the black man, incarnations of sentimentalized version of slavery. And what is worth observing also is that the Negro, with his quick, intuitive understanding of what is required of him, bodied them forth so convincingly that his masters were insulated against all questions as to their reality—were enabled to believe in them as honestly as they believed in so many other doubtful things.[12]

Faulkner's climate of consciousness may be tokenly suggested by other works. Here we may be merely briefly illustrative. There were works that concluded that Negroes were of the human species, but more like the monkey tribes and the lower order of animals than any other race. In the backwash of emotions engendered by the Southern drive for white supremacy, R. W. Shufeldt in 1907 published *The Negro, A Menace to Civilization,* a work which describes Negroes as the group most like the ape and lower animals— restrained from criminality only by fear of vicious bodily harm.[13] Shufeldt's whites represent reason developed to its highest point. But he sees the Black male as a rapist, whose habit is to enlarge the white female's "genital fissure" with a knife, in order that his great penis may be sufficiently accommodated. The mulatto, because of his white blood, may occasionally achieve, but he is dangerous since he possesses black criminal tendencies without the forewarning that black skin affords. Further, the mulatto sometimes passes into the white group and injects black blood, and by a throwback, coal black babies have been born to "white" couples who had reason to believe that they were free of black blood. The notion that black blood will out had appeared in less virulent form in *Uncle Tom's Cabin* and in Mark Twain's *Pudd'n Head Wilson.* It appears also in Faulkner's *Light in August,* in the voice of Gavin Stevens.

But in the early Twentieth Century, Thomas Dixon Jr.'s *The Leopard's Spots* had also made a "thing" of black blood. The liberal Bostonian Everett Lowell rejects the request of Negro George Harris, to be permitted to court Lowell's daughter: Lowell happens to "know" that black blood, even a century removed, will "suddenly breed back to a pure Negro child, thick lipped, kinky headed,

173

flat nosed, black skinned."[14] ". . . one drop of your blood in my family could push it backward three thousand years in history," Dixon has the liberal Lowell to exclaim. Most of Faulkner's rational statements deny the belief in race blood, but his imaginative statements create at least a credibility gap.

Such was the cultural collective unconscious (and conscious), with which Faulkner could make terms but he did so in his own way, and the pressure of mythic responses to Blackness can be found in many of his novels. Faulkner's imagination concerning Blacks was much closer to that of a non-contemporary, Thomas Jefferson, a reluctant critic of Blacks. Jefferson advanced it as a suspicion only, "that the Blacks, whether originally a distinct race, or made distinct by time and circumstances, are inferior to whites in the endowments of both body and mind."[15] Their imagination is "dull, tasteless, and anomalous," and they are much inferior to whites in reason, appearing to be in their existence "more of sensation than reflection." Negroes "are transient in grief, ardent after their female, but their love is without the tender delicate mixture of sentiment and sensation." Like Faulkner's Isaac in "The Bear," Jefferson credits Negroes with numerous instances of "benevolence, gratitude, and unshaken fidelity." Espeically has nature endowed him with heart—also bravery, adventuresomeness, and numerous instances of rigid integrity. However, the cold issue is that intermixture with whites will stain the blood of the masters; therefore, "When freed, he is to be removed beyond the reach of mixture."

While down at the ranch—Faulkner. In "A Word to Virginians," a speech delivered at the University of Virginia, Faulkner begins cautiously and tentatively.[16] Perhaps "the Negro is not yet capable of more than second-class citizenship. His tragedy may be that so far he is competent for equality only in the ratio of his white blood." So how is the Negro's freedom to be achieved? White men of the South must teach them to be "worthy" of freedom, a process involving the Blacks learning to think like the best of white men and ceasing "forever more thinking like a Negro and acting like a Negro. . . ." Negroes may not learn their a-b-c's or common fractions; but they must learn "the hard things—self restraint, honesty, dependability, purity; to act not even as well as any white man, but to act as well as the best of white men."

The imagery of Faulkner's speech is interesting and filled with the pressure of myth from his unconscious. The Negroes are 500 unbridled horses," whom whites will have to spend the rest of their lives dodging if the whites do not train them. Faulkner also speaks of five-thousand cats among five hundred unassimilated dogs, "or vice versa." Embarrassed under questioning from University students, Faulkner explained the horses image as a "quick analogy," at one point, and as an "unfortunate simile," at another, used because it was familiar. Then—other apologetic statements. (In his novel *Satoris,* an early work in complete agreement with the popular Southern white consciousness, Faulkner had found a strong resemblence between the Negro and the mule). Clearly, mythic assumptions peep from behind ostensibly rational statements. Below the level of consciousness old emotions and images roll, whirl, and play hang with the angularities of rational thought.

Jefferson would avoid impending miscegenation by physical colonization of Negroes "beyond the reach of mixture," Faulkner, by a colonization within the mind. On the one hand, Faulkner states that Negroes will disappear in five hundred years: ". . . and I imagine then anyone that wants to join the DAR will have to prove that she's got somewhere a strain of Negro blood, that they'll be descendants of . . . but as—I think as the NAACP preaches it, and as the White Citizens Councils preach against it, it won't occur. . . ." In the two statements, there is a contradiction more apparent than real. Faulkner would first have Blacks super-saturated with Anglo-Saxon puritanism, a process which would eventuate in their becoming super-white men in everything but color. Obviously, since there would no longer be "Negroes," there would be no reality in the question of mixing.

Asked to face the question of mixing in such blunt rhetoric, contemporary liberalism will probably recoil. This means that they fail to face their own mythic projections when stated in plain terms, since Faulkner's whitened "black" Anglo-Saxon is precisely the image of the popular white consciousness. It is up-dated in the recent film, "Guess Who's Coming to Dinner," in which the purported "Negro" male, who is to be awarded the Anglo-Saoxn female (after some soap-opera agonizing by the Anglo-Saxon family) is really, except for his black skin, Faulkner's super-Anglo-Saxon. First to be jettisoned from the white consciousness is the symbol of the black male as gross sexual potency: an intimate white mother-daughter chat reveals that the heroine has had an impulse to abandon her purity prematurely to the black hero—but the hero has been impervious, and has enforced upon the heroine a proper restraint. Then the super middle class symbols: the hero is an assistant professor of medicine at an English University and is known for highly significant medical research, and he will not marry the girl without parental approval. Compare Faulkner: Negroes "have got to compel the white people to say, Please come and be equal with us." So the family awards him the white female—a girl having the emotional quality of an arrested adolescent. The Black father, the only real Negro in the picture, i.e., the only person in touch with history, ideology, and the actual dynamics of American society, tries to say that he has not spent his life accumulating mileage as a postman for such an outcome. The father's trouble, the black son sternly points out, is that he thinks of himself as a Negro, whereas the son thinks of himself as an *individual*. (Universalism.) Suddenly, the movie has a real issue. The American system institutionalizes the individualism for whites while, simultaneously, regarding Blacks, it institutionalizes the oppression on the basis of group identity. So what public reality has the hero's rhetorical assertion of individuality? The movie solves the problem by quickly and permanently upstaging the father, and the hero and the audience are permitted to feel that they have dealt firmly with a major issue of American life and reaffirmed the humanistic content of Anglo-Saxon culture. So goes Western abstract univarlism.

As to Faulkner's Blacks, the first warning bell against making big announcements regarding their being defined in his fiction sounds definitively when we realize that we must mine them largely through the consciousness of the white characters. That is, we must first understand the white character's tensions and sickness of consciousness. In such early works as *Soldier's Pay* and *Sartois,* Faulkner's own consciousness and prejudices even in rational statements in the novels are clearly those of his white characters, so there's no great job to be done in assigning to most of them their mythic role in the validation of whiteness. Under the shocks of clock time and the First World War, the whites experienced an emasculation of the pioneer Southern aristocratic ideal, a basic element in their cultural compulsive. They are crumbling in this world of clock time. The faithful servants, black mammies, train porter, and yard men, are present to perform the ritual and mythic function of providing, in a world where time erodes and decays, a timeless and indestructible Eden. In *Soldier's Pay* the black mammy Aunt Callie eliminates her grandson's impulse to individuality and universal manhood by a single rebuke. In *Sartois,* Old Bayard Sartoris eliminates the crude gestures toward individuality and universal manhood of black Caspey Strother by socking it to him with a stick of wood. Blacks must remain outside clock time and society's guarantees—as they really do throughout the works of Faulkner.

If we are to understand Blacks in Faulkner's fiction, we must keep alert to what tends to tone the definition of man in Faulkner and in American culture. The pressure of rational ordering and some sort of exemplification of the individual life as the expression of revolutionary will, are important for the white heroes. The guy takes charge or explains why or is given some compensating revolutionary gesture. Embracing directly "universal" forces, the character deals, along with his individuality and uniqueness, with his inescapable orphanage in the universe. With the exception of Lucas Beauchamp of "The Fire in the Hearth" and "Intruder in the Dust," who is more of smokescreen than a reality, the role of representing Man, in this culturally conditioned sense, is reserved for the white consciousness. A Thomas Sutpen in *Absalom, Absalom!* effects a personal revolution" from the life of a poor white mountaineer to that of a powerful Southern planter. An L. Q. C. McCaslin in "The Bear" creates a plantation out of the wilderness, although his life is saturated with moral ambiguity. Even Mink Snopes of *The Mansion* is permitted to hold himself together in defiance of Time's manipulations and erosions, until he can exact his version of justice from his enemy Flem Snopes, and Boon Hogganbeck in "The Bear" jerks his being uptight in his love of the mongrel lion and in the slaughter of old Ben, the huge bear.

No, I'm not forgetting the characters whose beings do not even momentarily come together, and yet occupy prestigious places in Faulkner's fiction. But so much print and analysis have been spent upon the foregoing men and the books in which they appear that one must touch bases with them. In themselves, they often appear to one, after he has escaped from the spell of Faulkner's hallucinatory prose, figures of adolescent fantasy. The wild Surpen niggers in

Absalom, Absalom! exist to exemplify Thomas Sutpen's revolutionary will, his natural Anglo-Saxon mastery of sons of darkness, and his own mythic image in the community. Through the eyes of the frustrated spinster, Rosa Coldfield, Sutpen's mulatto daughter Clytemnestra appears as a nature image and faithful servant, and through the eyes of Quentin Compson comes apotheosis reserved for those Blacks who have given their all for the whites. Other than the Blacks mentioned we have the tragic no-nation mulattos. But since they are all seen through the white consciousness, the reader gets no idea of their *otherness.* They remain a thought that the white folks think, sometimes dramatizing the inner weather of whites by being seen watching the whites with "dark, unscrutable eyes."

As we leave the white characters who express revolutionary will exerted upon the physical world, we come to the more modern heroes who cannot get themselves together, and the proffered solution is apparent only. They are creatures who seem trapped in their whiteness. They have the ritual gestures of the Southern white consciousness, but the gestures no longer come with inevitability from the center of their beings. A Quentin Compson of *The Sound and the Fury* commits suicide, but an Isaac McCaslin of "The Old People" and "The Bear" will typify more efficiently the struggles of such heroes.

Isaac represents the negative possibilities of Western individualism. From his first appearance in the short story, "The Old People," he evidences an intense neutralizing, and therefore, crippling self-consciousness, although its ills are not fully apparent until the moment of crucial choice: the decision as to what constitutes a viable relationship to his Southern white heritage. In "The Old People" and in the first three parts of "The Bear," Faulkner plunges the reader into a fascinationg poem about nature and religious consciousness. The rhetoric is frequently spellbinding, and the reader forgets, until moments of reflection to ask what kind of boy is this Isaac who never plays in that unself-conscious animal way of boys, but hangs around adults and takes them with an open-mouth seriousness. He has the deadly seriousness of a middle-aged man. After learning deep things about nature and beauty, he leaves the fabled role in the Big Woods ands attempts to carry values into society. In the World of Nature, the Negro-Indian Sam Fathers was his spiritual father; but for entry in society, his white racist cousin McCaslin Edmonds is his spiritual father. Too few critics have noted that his second father prevails, and that Isaac does not really gainsay the racist arguments of his cousin. After recoiling initially from his discovery that his Grandfather L. Q. C. McCaslin begat a female child by his favorite slave's wife and then begat a child by his mulatto female offspring, Isaac is a mouthful of agonized puritanical rhetoric. His gesture of renouncing his plantation heritage is morally ambiguous, since he continues to receive from it a subsistence income. His remaining gestures and views are a recoil back to the most dyed in the wool Southern tradition. But reading Faulkner's rational statements, and not his imagery and tensioned situations, critics have held up Isaac as the representative of Faulkner's great moral vision. It should not be surprising that the Blacks reflected through Isaac's white consciousness fall into three rather standard categories: The Rousseauistic myth of Nature; the myth of blacks as deluded children; and the images of malignant nature wherever Isaac's tensioned being touches upon Reconstruction.

We may close with remarks concerning two characters for the creation of which Faulkner has been credited with great achievement: the black characters Dilsey Gibson of *The Sound and the Fury* and Lucas Beauchamp of "The Fire and the Hearth" and *Intruder in the Dust*. The truth is that both characters are narcissistic tributes to the old order of Southerners, to which Faulkner was committed. After extracting oneself from the engaging tentacles of Faulkner's highly tensioned rhetoric, it is rather chilling to realize that Dilsey's problems, as they are outlined by Faulkner, would have been solved by the existence of a good old aristocratic white master! A good deal has been made of Faulkner's magnanimity in portraying Dilsey as living in a world of eternal values, whereas her white masters are timebound and decaying. Since whites had seized the world and Dilsey has no real choice, the proposition is silly. Further, the Christian religion, as Frantz Fanon has so aptly pointed out in relationship to the colonized native, has not called Dilsey simply to the ways of God, but to "the ways of the white man, of the master, of the oppressor."[17] Thus Faulkner, since he does not engage the *otherness* of Dilsey—the complex relations to self and family which he would have to confront by taking a walk on a real black night from the big house to the cabin, and doing some sneaky listening there, is unable to give a sound psychological analysis of her motivation, although her status as a major character demands it. Instead, in the last part of *The Sound and the Fury,* Faulkner overwhelms us by emotionally charged scenes and arranging Dilsey's canonization. He substitutes, that is, apotheosis where analysis is required. By Faulkner's neglect of Dilsey's *otherness,* we are reminded of a statement by a Professor Jessie W. Parkinhurst, in an essay entitled "The Role of the Black Mammy in the Plantation Household," *Journal of Negro History,* July, 1938: "Most often her real name was not known, it was a matter of no significance." After all those pages devoted to something black called Dilsey, alas, we must still say that nobody knows her name.[18]

As to the Black Lucas Beauchamp, he is very simply Faulkner's myth of the Blacks, described in his speech "A Word to Virginians," who is gradually learning to think and act "like the best of white men," and to cease "forever more thinking and acting like a Negro. . . ." That is, the price of Lucas's stride toward freedom in his saturation in Anglo-Saxonism and worship of his white ancestors. One needs only to disregard Faulkner's purely rational statements and take, instead, his deeply felt imaginative imagery in order to see where things are really at. Example: Lucas has "Syriac features," and his face is the "composite tintype of ten-thousand undefeated Confederate soldiers. . . ." He rejects "not only Negro behavior . . . but country Negro behavior. . . ." He does not indulge in Negro Saturday nights, but, like the white planters, comes to town during the week, and wears the "once expensive black broadcloth suit . . . the raked fine hat . . . the heavy watchchain and the gold toothpick," like the white boy's (Charles Mallison's) own grandfather "had carried in his upper vest." Now Faulkner says that Lucas has mastered both his white and his black blood, but his imaginative statement clearly shows that Lucas's claim to dignity is based upon his having a white grandfather, Lucius Quintus Carothers McCaslin, and blood kinship to the descendants of his grandfather. In "The Fire and the Hearth" and in the novel *Intruder in the Dust,* Faulkner allows Lucas to make the local white folks look real bad. That's because they are present-day white folks. If we read carefully, we will find that Lucas is actually a glorification of the *Old-time* white folks, the plantation founders and plantation paternalism. Any study of the original typescripts in the Library of the

University of Virginia will make the situation clear. There Lucas says "sir," and has an imaginary conversation with one of the white old-timers in which Lucas addresses him as "Old Master," an expression which Faulkner carefully emended, but Lucas as a great tribute to the old South and its paternalism remains.

Faulkner's *Intruder in the Dust* has its fantastic plot, not merely because it is an attempt at a detective story, but because it has so little relationship to the reality which it purports to describe. For the truth is that Lucas Beauchamp, in the lynch-minded South that Faulkner is dealing with, would have lost first the great symbol—his testicles, and then his life. Anyone doubting that Lucas would have perished violently needs only to study Arthur Raper's analysis of lynching and racial violence.[19] A fantastic plot allows Lucas's survival. It allows the white boy Chick Mallison, the modernized version of Huck Finn, to give final paternalistic approval of Lucas's potentiality for becoming white. And it allows the turgid rhetoric of Gavin Stevens to drug the basic alienation of Chick Mallison, and drive the plot to a mere ceremonial conclusion.

Intruder in the Dust represents the attainment of a high point of sickness in the works of Faulkner.

Unless one separates this sickness from his real achievement, all is blurred.

Yet beneath all the white nationalism, the symbolic needs concreted in black characters, and the sickness, real achievement lies. It lies both in Faulkner's ambivalent and ambiguous representation of Blacks and in a like representation of white Western cultural compulsives. His achievement lies least in the extended portraits of black characters, although, along with their roles as massagers of white symbolic needs and narcissistic compliments to a mythic Old Order of Whites, they do tell us important things about the weight of whiteness upon them and about the tough fiber that subserved a non-rational adjustment to the non-rational universe to which they were confined. Faulkner has a deep sense of that, although its mining was confined to the Big House, shored up by only a few peeping glances toward the desperations of the cabin.

His strong achievement with black characters is really those minor personalities that suddenly pop up rock-like and ambiguous, with stories that are at once adumbrated and truncated: an anonymous black farmer in *Sartoris* facing at midnight a disordered young white aristocrat who might just carelessly burn down the black man's barn; several ex-slaves in the fourth part of "The Bear," scattered minor characters in *The Sound and the Fury* and in *Light in August,* the anonymous mulatto mistress of Roth Edmonds in "Delta Autumn," etc., characters that make brief appearances, stand for a second in a sea of white and abruptly disappear, after demonstrating the stubborness and ambiguity of their lives. Faulkner's fiction would be poorer without them, and no major white writer has said more with more, but the comparison is in a limited field.

Faulkner's greater achievement is his white nationalism: A bemoaning of the demise of Western cultural compulsives, upon which he alternately casts a despairing eye and clutches to his bosom. He is the poet of disintegration. If one wishes to catch the pure funeral chant of these ceremonies of death, besides which his Nobel prize speech is a boy scout oration, one should begin with *Light in August* where key white characters clutch for their symbolic Negro as Yoknapotawpha crumbles in the dying strains of Faulkner's music. The ceremonies of *The Sound and the Fury* and *Absalom, Absalom!* then gain a greater articulation in the same direction.

And now, at the end, what can we finally say of the cultural compulsives and cultural imposition? We can certainly say that an understanding of their role relieves Blacks of the weigthy pronouncements of white Faulknerian critics—and those of their black followers. We can identify the real Faulknerian moments and the real Faulknerian situations in which black life is caught with some intensity and complexity, and we are prepared to see the essential pathos of the white condition and to step back from its area of sickness.

FOOTNOTES

1. *Black Skins, White Masks* (New York, 1967), p. 188.
2. "Of Our Spiritual Strivings," *The Souls of Black Folks* (New York, 1961), pp. 16-17.
3. "Art and Social Change," *Modern Quarterly* (Winter, 1937), p. 16. See also 16-127.
4. William Faulkner, *The Yoknapatawpha Country* (New Haven, 1963), pp. 334, 341. Brooks allows for cultural significance in an *incidental* way.
5. "Come Back to the Raft Ag'in, Huck Honey," *Partisan Review* 15 (June, 1948), pp. 669-670.
6. Allardyce Nicoll, ed., Shakespeare Survey 17, (Cambridge, 1965), pp. 37-52.
7. "The Compulsive Basis of Social Thought," *American Journal of Sociology* 36 (March, 1931), p. 591.
8. *Ibid.*, here and there, pp. 689-720.
9. Thomas Y. Gossett, *Race, The History of an Idea in America* (New York, 1965).
10. *Absalom, Absalom!* (New York, 1951), p. 89. Reference is to the Modern Library edition.
11. Franklin L. Riley, ed., *Publications of the Mississippi Historical Society*, Vol. 13, pp. 223-271..
12. W. J. Cash, *The Mind of the South* (New York, 1941), pp. 86-87.
13. *The Negro, A Menace to Cililization* (Boston, 1907).
14. Thomas Dixon, Jr., *The Leopard's Spots* (Ridgewood, N. J.), p. 398.
15. *Notes on the State of Virginia* (New York, 1964), pp. 138, 132-139.
16. *Faulkner in the University* (New York, 1959), p. 210, pp. 209-227.
17. *The Wretched of the Earth* (New York, 1966), p. 34.
18. "The Role of the Black Mammy in the Plantation Household," *Journal of Negro History* 23 (July, 1938), p. 356.
19. Arthur Raper, *The Tragedy of Lynching* (Chapel Hill, 1933).

Before Ideology:
Reflections on Ralph Ellison
and the Sensibility
of Younger Black Writers

THAT SOME YOUNGER BLACK WRITERS AND RALPH Ellison sharply and fundamentally disagree in ideology and artistic perspective is not, on its face, alarming. Such an outcome is par for the course when a new generation arrives, seeking answers to age old problems in the light of current rhythms of reality. Then, too, in the arts, the revolt of the next generation is the rule rather than the exception.

The crucial question is whether the ensuing disagreement, preclude both sides from absorbing from each other. Ideally, younger writers, while revolting, absorb angles of vision and techniques from older writers, and older writers absorb certain of the tensions provided by the younger—not necessarily changing techniques or vision, but accommodating within them the urgency of prevailing insights and tensions. Without abandoning her habitual humanistic high ground, Gwendolyn Brooks, it seems to me, has effected a healthy and stimulating relationship with young radical writers in Chicago. On the one hand, they write better because of her, and on the other, many of the tensions that they respond to are confronted in her book *In the Mecca*.

But perhaps in such a rough and tumble situation as the artistic process represents, one can not hope for many "ideal" relationships. Perhaps what can be more easily available is the highly tensioned relationship that seems to have characterized the James Baldwin-

Richard Wright pattern, as Baldwin describes it in *Nobody Knows My Name*. For whatever one makes out of Baldwin's twistings and turnings regarding Wright's achievement (both in *Notes of a Native Son* and *Nobody Knows My Name*), it is apparent that even his disagreement with Wright was a productive process.

In the case of Ellison and some younger black writers, it is precisely the threat that disagreements will rigidify into unproductiveness that gives cause for alarm. Ellison is charged with a bill of indictments that runs from abandonment of younger writers to representing a tortuous irrelevance, and from Ellison, himself, come comments that seem to add up to the proverbial flag waved in the face of a bull. Thus in calling attention to James Alan McPherson's *Hue and Cry* on its book-jacket, Ellison speaks of McPherson as promising to pass by immediately "those talented and misguided writers of Negro American cultural background who take being black as a privilege for being obscenely second-rate and who regard their social predicament as Negroes as exempting them from the necessity of mastering the craft and forms of fiction," and describes McPherson's stories as "a hue and cry against the dead, publicity-sustained writing which has come increasingly to stand for what is called black writing. . . ."

Now at stake in all this are not only Ellison and other talented writers, but nothing less than what may be the last opportunity to establish a tradition in black writing which is capable of rendering the complexity, density, and variety of the black experience. For despite the number of talented people who have made contributions to an interpretation of black experience and character, youngsters seeking concepts of themselves are still unwittingly drawn into accepting some of the flattest and most sterile categories provided by sociology. And I don't mean that sociology is the unrelenting enemy of literature, since a hostile relationship between the two seems inevitable only when the writer does not properly digest the sociology and form through his own kind of discovery images powerful enough to impose upon culture the illusion that he has conquered the density and contradictoriness of "reality."

Black literature is still in the state of not having absorbed at depth either its folk or general cultural tradition, an area where Ellison has much to tell us. This absorption of what existed in white literary tradition that could be called "folk" has been evidenced by such major American writers as Nathaniel Hawthorne, Mark Twain, and Faulkner, not to mention an assorted group of local colorists and regionalists from all areas of America who frequently surfaced the material which major writers were to turn to greater account. But in black folk tradition, although the blues and spiritual areas have received considerable attention, the symbolic potential of the supernatural as reflected in ghost stories, conjure pieces, and unusual happenings, has yet to receive full exploitation.

Langston Hughes, of course, made sorties into the area of the supernatural—or the area of fantasy bordering upon it, his most notable effort being the brilliant one-act play, "Soul Gone Home." Henry Dumas, a young writer reportedly killed by New York police in May, 1968, made promising explorations in such stories as "Rain God" (*Negro Digest,* January, 1968), "Will the Circle Ever be Broken," (*Negro Digest,* November, 1966), and "Fon" (Black Fire, 1968). A few others have made sorties.

Further, one can still read so much of black literature without discovering that despite those images of the "emasculated male" and the "matriarch" black men and women have loved each other. Charles Chesnutt in his short story "Po' Sandy" (*The Conjure Woman,* 1899) long ago used the conjure tradition to describe a passionate affair between a slave and his wife. Chestnutt's symbols vibrate with more resonance than many of the current attempts to describe passionate commitments, some of which seem to project more of their proximity to the white "sexual revolution" than to any deep concept of love. But despite the foregoing examples, the tradition is relatively unexploited.

The same conclusion applies to sermons and church rituals. Then we may move out of folk tradition and apply the same conclusion to the little noted resource of autobiography, which frequently merely shadows forth the shorthand of a complexity which a writer of fiction would be better equipped to develop. The most complex picture of miscegenation, for example, is not in Faulkner, but in Pauli Murray's autobiographical narrative, *Proud Shoes,* a work that should long ago have been reprinted. Both Frederick Douglass's *Narrative* and *The Autobiography of Malcolm X* contain transformation-into-manhood episodes, which, in the hands of a talented black novelist, should become the nucleus of very great scenes indeed. Then back to the black man-black woman situation: while describing civil rights activities in his autobiography, *Nigger,* Dick Gregory tells of a Mississippi black farmer, briefly imprisoned for killing a man whom whites had sent to kill him, whose only regret is that the wife from whom he had never been separated for an entire day died while he was in prison. He also tells the rather moving story of a deserting father. Both require the definition and sense of discovery which can be provided only by the imaginative artist. Finally, it is in Mrs. Medgar Ever's autobiographical statement *For Us the Living* that we have outlined in the beginning chapters the struggle of one black woman to disengage herself from the comfort sensibility provided by American culture, in order to relate to a rather tough-minded black man's version of the expression of manhood.

But in black fiction perhaps the most powerful analysis of man and woman's intimate relationship to each other may well be Chester Himes's *Third Generation,* in which the intimacy is one reached through a most terrible hatred.

Before ideology. . . .

People before ideology—the problem of defining the complexity, density and variety of black people. For whatever purpose black people are to come together, this matter of deep definition would seem to be a primary matter. Certainly, if we are to be launched into that terrifying and unpredictable future known as revolution, it would seem not enough for us to be defined in relationship to white men and women. We must also see ourselves in relationship to those terrible rhythms that work at our depth, whose survival of the fire may be termed beautiful.

What I've been trying to suggest so far is that the necessity for black tradition to truly mine the complexity, density, and variety of black experience, and the people who exist before the tortuous shapes that ideologies take, whether high ground traditional humanism or revolutionary, hardly leave us with the privilege of blowing to the winds techniques and insights derivable from a diversity of viewpoints. In the interest of this position, I should like to offer notes on the sensibilities of Ellison and radical writers. My motive is to outline the shaping areas, so that depths may be looked upon and disagreements made there. Once men can agree to disagree and yet recognize a common impulse, it is possible that they may find ways in which their currents can serve each other.

By sensibility I mean the writer's equipment for interpreting existence, those psychic, intellectual, emotional, and feeling patterns that seem to comprise his characteristic response to the currents of life. In the case of Ellison, we have fragments of reviews, complete essays, interviews, his short stories, and his novel *Invisible Man,* in which to find its reflection. But the primary focus here is what may be loosely called his *racial* sensibility.

The whole framework created by Ellison reveals a carefully built edifice from which his thinking and fiction are projected. One very important fact about the Ellison framework is that its design was probably completed during the early 1940's. In the August 5, 1941 review of black writing for the *New Masses,* he praises Richard Wright for approaches and responses to American reality and to black life, especially for seizing the big picture of American life, building up within himself the taut tensions implied by the American ethos, translating that ethos into the terms of Bigger Thomas's life, and operating boldly as a conscious artist. Wright is seen as one who has stolen the fire, since he has snatched the techniques, the cultural skills, and the broad view from the horizon, usually reserved for whites.[1] Thus Ellison is celebrating in another's achievements goals that he has adopted for himself. The thing to do, both on practical and idealistic grounds, was to invade the territory of the conquerors and beat them by their own rules.

The above definition of the field of battle and the champion's stance is characteristic of Ellison's sensibility today, it is also interesting to note that he was addicted to it during the earlier 1930's period when he was still planning to win his place in music. In *Indivisible Man* (*Atlantic,* December, 1970), he says: "And here I was with a dream of myself writing the symphony at twenty-six which would equal anything Wagner had done at twenty-six." At the time, Ellison was uneasily involved with in-laws, who thought he lacked ambition because he did not accept a job with the post-office.[2]

Ellison's book reviews of the 1940's period, and sometimes earlier, merit study because they reveal artistic principles which his sensibility had assimilated and perspective regarding his concept of the relationship between black culture and American culture in general. In "Recent Negro Fiction," he stated that techniques were both reflections and instruments of consciousness—that is, the techniques must be the effective rendering of the complexity of one's awareness. In his review of William Attaway's *Blood on the Forge*,[3] he criticized the lack of a Jamesian center of consciousness, capable of understanding the events of the book. Other criticisms imply, sometimes in a single sentence of a review, technical considerations that were part of his own framework: that black writers frequently adopted techniques without understanding the assumptions behind them; that in a novel all questions of reality are to be confronted; that a tempo and procedure suitable to the novel can be sluggish in the drama; that the artist's job is to brood over the experience he perceives until it takes a meaningful shape within his mind, etc.

During the 1940's also, Ellison, as reflected in his review of Langston Hughes's progress and a seminal essay on Richard Wright ("Richard Wright's Blues"), came to precise terms with the signification that folk forms bear and can be made to bear. At the same time, he was taking pains to identify the myth-making tendencies and strategic ignorance of the white mind which distort folklore, black life, and black and white relations. And he had sensed at depth the symbolic and psychological needs which laid heavy and guiding hands upon the minds of whites.

Now I am not trying to suggest that Ellison's perceptions were unique, but that he brought them into precise and usable relationship to an artist's workshop. James Weldon Johnson had much earlier stressed the need for folk forms and dialect to express blacks from within. Alain Locke, particularly in his essay on Sterling Brown's *Southern Road* (a work that should have been reprinted long ago), spoke incisively about truly meaningful uses of folk tradition. In "Sterling Brown: The New Negro Folk Poet," included in Nancy Cunard's anthology *Negro,* Locke stressed the importance of a *deep idiom of feeling* and *thought* native to the historical spread of black tradition, which he found in Brown's work. Other writers had commented upon both folk tradition and the psychology of race relations, but it seems to me that Ellison shaped these insights into a tool for writers, and, with respect to folk and cultural tradition attempted to define both its utility and its limits.

In such 1940's essays as "Harlem Is Nowhere" and "An American Dilemma: A Review," reprinted in *Shadow and Act*, Ellison examines a folk personality bereft of its traditional institutional supports and confronted by sophisticated institutional vibrations in the modern city that remained aloof or subtly destructive to its basic needs. Ostensibly, a discussion of a psychiatric clinic devoted to the needs of urban Blacks, "Harlem Is Nowhere," in the process of describing the terrible dilemma of the migrant, makes the existence of the clinic a beautiful irrelevancy. Ellison wills to see Harlem "as not merely the scene of the folk-Negro's death agony," but "the setting of his transcendence." That is, for the migrant's children, Harlem can become the source of self-realization. Metaphor, however, heavily weights the negative: "In relation to their Southern background, the history of Negroes in the North reads like the legend of some tragic people out of mythology, a people which aspired to escape from its own unhappy homeland to the apparent peace of a distant mountain; but which, in migrating, made some fatal error of judgment and fell into a great chasm of maze-like passages that promise ever to lead to the mountain but end ever against a wall."

Ellison's review of Gunnar Myrdal's *An American Dilemma,* written for but not published in the *Antioch Review,* does not emphasize the folk directly. But after acknowledging the positive contribution of Myrdal and identifying the racism of earlier approaches to Blacks by the social sciences, Ellison pointed out a major limitation of Myrdal's work: his view of Negro culture and personality as simply a product of social pathology. Thus Myrdal's science, Ellison stated, was not deep enough to analyze what was happening among Blacks and provided for an assimilation into American culture on white terms only. What was needed was for Black and white to work for a change in the *basis* of the society, and Negroes to create from Negro culture the uncreated consciousness of their race.

It was also during the 1940's that Ellison indirectly suggested the importance of seeing the artistic possibilities of black life through the lens provided by the great masters, some evidence of which may be found in "Richard Wright's Blues," and "Harlem Is Nowhere." Permeating all his statements is the emphasis which he gives to the Americanness of all positions and his engagement with all strands of the American cultural fabric.

Ellison's sensibility thus takes its mold from his struggles to perceive during the 1940's and earlier; subsequent statements are largely expansions and more detailed descriptions of this sensibility. Thus what might appar to be a merely humorous statement which appears in the 1970 interview, *Indivisible Man,* (*Atlantic Monthly,* December), is really quite significant. There, in response to Leslie Fielder's having dismissed him as a black Jew, Ellison says that "someone should have said that *all* us old-fashioned Negroes are Jews." As Ellison, I think, would admit (see his compariosn of the situations of Jewish and Black writers in "A Very Stern Discipline," *Harper's,* March, 1967), the Black-Jew analogy breaks down real fast.[4] But I believe that what he had in mind was the style of taking the rules of the game created by the opponent for his own benefit and overwhelming him with sheer energy, cunning, desperate skill, and intensity of competition.

It should be admitted that this style is an intrinsic aspect of black tradition. It has characterized all those Blacks who, throughout American history, suddenly jumped forth from nowhere to take command of the scene—black abolitionists, the early W. E. B. Du-Bois, a tidal wave of black athletes, etc. Bereft of one's own gods with which to turn the tide, the individual black man was forced to do battle in a social arena and to seize individually upon Western gods (Christianity, reason, high culture, the Bill of Rights, the Constitution, the fleet foot) and attempt to turn their cutting edge upon the opponent. After this mad dash up flight after flight of stairways (the elevators being reserved for whites), however comes the harder thing: one must now ritually affirm the value of the gods and the game, make the testimony of faith, that is, that the game's intrinsic beauty is its own excuse for being. At one point, the young W. E. B. DuBois, who was yet to go through many changes, after painting a rugged picture of the crosses of black life that must have strained the outer limits of his sensibility, expressed the true ritual of the faith:

> I sit with Shakespeare and he winces not. Across the color line I move arm in arm with Balzac and Dumas, where smiling men and welcoming women glide in *guilded* halls. From out the caves of evening that swing between the strong-limbed earth and the tracery of the stars, I summon Aristotle and Aure-

lius and what soul I will, and they come all graciously with no scorn or condescension. So, wed with truth, I dwell above the veil. Is this the life you grudge us, O Knightly America? Is this the life you long to change into dull red hideousness of Georgia? Are you so afraid lest peering from this high Pisgah, between Phillistine and Amalekite, we sight the Promised Land? [5]

DuBois's words are possibly the classic statement of personal resolution through seizure of the traditional humanistic high ground of Western culture, a resolution through the achievement of *private* and *individual* reality. In the same book, *The Souls of Black Folks,* however, he was to become ambivalent about the death of his infant son in the chapter, "The Passing of the First Born." Was it a good or bad thing? The son would not face soul-searing humiliations from his native land, the kind that bugged the proud DuBois. Yet, might not the son have borne his burden more skillfully than the father? And is not time to be believed in as the bringer of the new and the more hopeful? Yes—a strained sensibility.

In the same work, the situation is not helped to assume a brighter face by DuBois's short story, "Of the Coming of John," in which the Western rituals of uplift, rationality, moral suasion, and individual heightening of consciousness, are painfully acted out—only to bring about estrangement between the black hero and the black community and his destruction through violence.

As DuBois describes the sudden destruction and, at best, slow attrition experienced by the ordinary black rural family near the turn of the Century, an experience which is at once an expense of soul and a source of it, one feels the continued strain upon his sensibility and the source of that impulse that eventually sought more complex explanations for the motives of men. Obviously, neither for the general black situation nor for the individual in *The Souls of Black Folks,* does the traditional high ground humanism provide a secure possession of the black self.

Despite the strained condition which I have attributed to high ground humanism I am after no simple conclusion that it was worthless. For it was wielded by gifted Blacks with a certain Brer' Rabbit wiliness, and some of the spirit and wit of High John de Conquer. And it has its notched scoreboard of half loaves, which one can ignore only if he insists upon rigidly holding his back to the past and his face to the front—a posture involving a petrified presentism. Still, the situation is so strained that it would seem that a tough-minded worker on the traditional humanistic high ground as represented by Ellison and those younger workers for various versions of revolutionary change and the definition of black people would be able to define a common ground.

The problem requires a respectful scrutiny of the new and younger sensibility. It arose following the peaking of the high ground approach that seemed to promise much, but instead forced upon consciousness pictures of an American and Western counter-rhythm which seemed to insure that the more things changed, the more they would remain the same—if not worse. The 1954 Supreme Court decision and subsequent decisions against segregation, the rise and fall of The Reverend Martin Luther King, the endless brutality and neutralization that surfaced as an inherent part of the system, the seemingly endless absorption of punishment by such organizations as the idealistic SNCC, the gassing at Selma Bridge, the James Meredith march and consequences, and the rebellions in the cities, seemed to force revelations about the state of the nation and its system that could not be blinked away. The bombing that killed the four black girls in the Birmingham church not only revealed the deep seated illness provided by racism, but critically wounded the generator of the high ground faith. One needs only to listen to the recorded ceremonies of the Albany Movement to realize that the black effort had required near exhaustion of all its reserves of religious principles and emotions.

Here so many of the old sustaining myths rapidly died. Perhaps the worst was faith in the relevance of individual white friendships when it was really the built-in rhythm of a system that was doing the work. Outside the dramatic brutality was a system involving automation and cybernation that not only seemed to write off a generation of black men, but to consign subsequent generations to a permanent place in the cellar. Worse still, with the diminished need for common labor, Blacks seemed an economic irrelevancy.

With such a system, a few Blacks could be allowed to slip through the barricades indefinitely without changing the status of the group or gaining fundamental dignity for themselves. Integration thus seemed to loom not as a real liberation, but simply as another system of control. When the young Black looked meditatively at the Western dispensation for Blacks across the world, he could hardly find reassurance. The workings of a very complex system of commercialism and technology seemed to be a trap for Blacks, even when situations had the label *freedom* conferred upon them. Of course, there were white men on the wrong side of this system, but neither the history of the labor movement nor the American and European response to Marx seemed to promise that whites would not continue to settle for bigger crumbs of the pie seasoned with a generous salting of white supremacy.

In the American and Western power to define and make definitions stick, an awakening young Black found a more subtle, dangerous, and nightmarish oppression. It meant that one had to consider whether one's whole reality system was indeed one's own —or imposed brutally or beneficently by the oppressor. It meant that whether you were a Bigger Thomas, the only Black in the newly integrated corporation, a university student, or even a revolutionist, long hands reached out to viciously slap or caress your reality into shape. It meant, possibly, that when you walked into the door of the newly integrated corporation you left the black self outside as a condition of admittance; that when you entered the university you confronted polite but highly systematized definitions of yourself which, when translated, signified that you were nothing in particular; that when you, as revolutionist, were deciding the time for revolution some agency's hands could just be guiding the black fingers that set the clock.

Despite the fact that young black men went out to shout and write about their discoveries of the perilous condition of black men as if they were entirely new perceptions, the resources for articulation of their sensibility extended from the present to the remote past. Some persons, of course, read sources more for therapy than for thought. Thus Frantz Fanon's justifications for violence were widely absorbed, but not, seemingly, his analysis of the limitations of spontaneous rebellion, his insistence upon a growth of consciousness that reached for a new humanistic ideal, and his insistence that some whites would find a genuine place in the revolution.[6] But gradually his total message got across—for acceptance, rejection, or adaptation.

Fanon could say: "All the elements of a solution to the great problems of humanity, have, at different times, existed in European thought." Of course, he went on to say: "But the actions of European men have not carried out the mission which fell to them, and which consisted of bringing their whole weight to bear violently upon these elements, of modifying their arrangements and their nature, of changing them and finally of bringing the problem of mankind to an infinitely higher plane."[7]

Fanon called for a new approach from the Third World, because the Western adventure had broken the unity of man, and among other activities, committed a genocide which set aside from the category of humanity "15,000 millions of men." And when he put aside theory and searched for Man in the "technique and style" of Europe, he could see "only a succession of negations of man and an avalanche of murders" both on Europe's own street corners and "in all corners of the globe." According to Fanon, the example of Europe was followed by America, and resulted in monstrosity.

There were of course the insights of many other non-Americans which aided the articulation of the new sensibility, but the home grown visions of several Blacks, past and present, were just as crucial, if not more crucial. Blacks' adamant and new insistence upon making their own definitions of men freed and opened their minds. Malcolm X, for example, could be to whites merely a dangerous agitator; defined in relationship to black realities he was a saint. Here was a man who had moved from a *knotted* to a *positive niggerhood*. Obviously, one can here hardly do more justice to his impact than to give it a name, for he literally called thousands of black men and women back to a new view of themselves and their situation. His existence validated the rhythms of a black reality, and provided for a positive view of large numbers of men who under the impulse for integration had been labeled criminals and consigned to garbage disposal units. In his own person, he seemed to embody the possibilities of a solid black manhood, and he was a magnet drawing the young back to those black communities from which they had fled, back to themselves, back home.

Now Muslims have rightfully resented a focus upon Malcolm X, which precludes appropriate credit to Elijah Muhammad, his spiritual father. For, without him and the Muslim movement there would have been no Malcolm X. My excuse is that I'm not trying to celebrate persons, but to describe the young black sensibility through its most immediate sources of articulation. This sensibility soon found itself encountering analyses authored by Blacks whose appearance on the American scene ranged in time from slavery to the present.

Out of all this has developed a very diverse movement in writing, as well as in life. It is a movement that ranges in its concerns from the simple demand that one be able to make whatever moves one wishes from a basis of identity to a devotion to various versions of revolution. Very valuable in helping the individual black person to hear himself above the din of outcries and to define where he, himself, is has been such works as Harold Cruse's *Crisis of the Negro Intellectual* and *Rebellion or Revolution,* with their insistence upon definition of stances and the absurdity of an anti-intellectual position.

The recognition of current black writing as being diverse is also a way of identifying its vulnerability. Thus almost any charge may be placed against it by picking on *one* aspect of its diversity, as do some black critics who come to it with the attitude of glimpsing quickly what *"they* are doing over *there."* Thus one can very quickly point out a verse in which the author seemed to have felt that three uses of the word motherfucker automatically and simultaneously create a poem and an instrument for liberation. There are probably too many poems that raise the question as to whether they could exist without whitey at the center, and, by sheer preoccupation with his qualities, create a reverse celebration. There is evidence also of wooden repetition of themes substituted for the necessary act of creative discovery, some stereotyping of approaches, and some unintended celebrations of Blackness on a merely *rhetorical* or *sloganeering* level. Besides facile adverse criticism, there is also praise that comes too simply.

But the trouble with this criticism is not that it blames or praises, but that it is not serious. It can not help us to know what to think of such diverse and flexible talents as those (to name a few) of Larry Neal in *Black Boogaloo,* who is as fine a poet as he is a critic; Don L. Lee, whose latest book *We Walk the Way of the New World* is both a measure of talent and continued growth; of LeRoi Jones, leader but not controller of the Black Arts Movement; Calvin Hernton, Sonia Sanchez, Etheridge Knight, A. B. Spellman,

196

Mari Evans, Carolyn Rogers, Nikki Giovanni—and others that might be named. It can not help one to understand even the diversity of the individual writer as he moves from book to book. The situation assumes greater momentousness because it is now at the point where it can benefit by a knowledgeable criticism.

It is also at a point where it might gather its forces to move more deeply into what I have been calling the density, variety, and complexity of the realities of black life. Surely, whatever move black people eventually decide to make, (and nobody can really name the move in advance), the availability of images of them that vibrate with a persistent resonance—that impose themselves upon culture as much as Bigger Thomas might be spoken of as an image imposed upon culture, will be crucial. But this time, black literature will be pressed to meet also the cry that is abroad for images of a *positive niggerhood*. I hope it is clear that the term *positive niggerhood* has nothing to do with simple respectability or chamber-of-commerce public relations: it has to do with catching up with public images of manhood and womanhood that have been produced across the years of black history, but have especially proliferated during the past twenty years. Such images have a defining power, and vibrate behind the consciousness of a writer without his trying to make an exact copy of them.

Having attempted to suggest that the sensibility of Ralph Ellison achieved its form during the 1940's, and having described younger writers as operating from a sensibility most responsive to the 1960's, it may, at first, seem odd that I continue to suggest that Ellison's resources would be useful in the push for further depth. But any notion of obsolescence derives from the failure to realize that the new thing about the new sensibility is not its material but its insistent focus and direction. If the new sensibility forgets that much of its materials are not brand new, it is in danger of patronizing the ordinary man whom it wishes to reach, and who, in the earlier absence of a comforting resource of a black consciousness of any considerable magnitude, could afford to retain the bitter dregs of his situation only sometimes in the mind. He who does not realize this knows or understands little of the black cultural and folkloric tradition.

As to Ellison, the major differences to be found reside in his ritual affirmation of faith in the West, his emphasis on cultural blending, and his exclusion of Africa as a psychological resource. There are, of course, other differences, but should they be permitted to remain insuperable obstacles? The simple fact is that *Shadow and Act* represents one of the deepest and most usable analyses of culture available to the writer, and some of its insights are to be found nowhere else. To take a single example: if one strips Ellison's review of *An American Dilemma* of its ritual affirmation of faith, one finds written in 1944 an analysis of institutional racism that no radical could better in 1971. If we move to *Invisible Man*, we are confronted with a work whose analysis of black life and tensions (along with its universalism) and whose powerful imaging have hardly been equalled.

Certainly some confusion regarding Ellison's achievement derives from his tendency to overstate his case when it touches upon a source of irritation: his identity, universalism, the sociological, etc. Thus in the 1955 Interview "The Art of Fiction," included in *Shadow and Act,* he compels a focus upon the novel's universalism by stating that the novel is not an attack upon white society. The novel is universal, but it is *also* a powerful attack on white society. One great value for the building of a deeper probing in black is Ellison's unsurpassed example of how much signification the self-conscious writer can force folklore and cultural tradition to bear in a self-conscious art. He celebrates the folklore potential in "The Art of Fiction," but when Stanley Edgar Hyman seemed in a 1958 speech on Negro Folk Tradition to confine the black writer's resources to his folklore, Ellison responded by correcting Hyman's view of folklore, insisting that the black writer's heritage of "the human experience which is literature" might be of primary importance, and slightly downgrading the importance of folk literature.

Ellison's differences with nationalists and students are more complicated. Some seem to be fundamental; others may be modifiable provided he had the kind of contact with them to allow himself to feel his way into their situations. In the 1970 interview essay that appears in the December issue of *Harper's* oversimplifications abound, some of which derive from James McPherson's statement of a question. Others derive from Ellison's having associations with certain terms that differ from those of a younger generation.

In contrast to the younger group, he seems to see "black awareness" not as a *process* of moving away from situations of under-valuation of self, but as simple narcissism, a denial of the intricacy with which Blackness is interwoven into the fabric of American culture. The tendency of black students to cluster together suggests a lack of confidence (unjustifiable) and a withdrawal from competition—a simplification of a rather complex situation. Ellison's concern, however, is that black students will miss the opportunity to influence the values that govern college campuses and step back from achievement. A fundamental question for many black writers is how to secure a black audience, for Ellison—how to make an impact upon the "broader community," which, of course, would not exclude attention to the black community. When he discusses the power of Booker T. Washington, one is not sure as to what degree he has faced the current question of "power for whom?"

In the 1967 *Harper's* interview, "A Very Stern Discipline," Ellison viewed the resentment that he (and other writers similarly situated) experienced from sections of the black community as explicable by the Booker Washington metaphor of the crabs in the basket who pull back the individual crab as he is about to escape.[8] The group's reaction, as suggested by the story, is protective—a heritage from slavery, in which the unpredictable actions of the individual are suppressed in order to insure the security of the group. James McPherson picks up Ellison's concept in the December, 1970 interview, "Indivisible Man," in attempting to explain reactions to Ellison in the current black movement. Here the reactions are called "the defense mechanism of the black community," "the impulse toward leveling," and the preference for the simplistic "right-on man of black slang."[9] In the light of the fact that the writers having reservations about Ellison are likely to be those involved in the complex sensibility that I have described and in a quest for goals which differ from Ellison's, the above explanation will be seen as rather simplistic.

In the following statement, McPherson perhaps unwittingly oversimplifies the diveristy of the black writing movement:

> Dear Ralph: There is a popular phrase, widely circulated now by militants, to the effect that the present "movement" cannot afford any individuals, that if you "are not part of the solution, you are part of the problem."

For the black writer, I assume this means that he cannot deal analytically with the complexities of black experience in fiction unless he asserts the current ideological thoughts of the group as construed by its "spokesmen."[10]

Now the fact is that the views of writers committed and uncommitted to what is known as the radical movement in black writing are liberally documented in the January, 1968 issue of *Negro Digest*.

The single essay in favor of McPherson's interpretation is Ron Karenga's "Black Art: A Rhythmic Reality of Revolution." I, myself, find Karenga's remarks rather chilling and an extremely tight box for the artist to dwell in. It has all the beauty and the unreality of the Western syllogism. Here Karenga calls for a black art that is *functional, collective,* and *committing,* attacks individuality, and states his concept of the usefulness of Black art: "Black Art must expose the enemy, praise the people and support the revolution."[11] Whatever Karenga's intention, it is rather difficult not to envision a cultural comissar arriving to enforce upon the artist his version of what fits the people's needs. Or perhaps the version of his superior or committee. James Cunningham in the same issue in "Ron Karenga and Black Cultural Nationalism, Hemlock for the Black Artist: Karenga Style" presents an able rebuttal, but ends up by recommending the "art for art's sake" tradition, which is too closely associated with the Western artist alienated from the community to be useful to the black artist who is trying to find his relationship to the community. Although Cunningham sees an exact equation between Karenga and LeRoi Jones (and Black Cultural Nationalism), no careful reading of Jones will suggest that he could be packaged in Karenga's box.

Of the thirty-two writers giving their statements on the writers' role in the same issue under the heading "Writers Symposium," the ten easily recognizable as cultural nationalists record a diversity of views. But I would particularly call attention to the statements of Laurence P. Neal, which certainly invite complexity of exploration of the black experience, chide black writers for not having exploited their historical and public figures, and remind them of such matters as the importance of the variety of folk and cultural forms and styles.[12] Ellison shares McPherson's misunderstanding and sees the current movement as repeating mistakes committed during the literary period of the 1930's.

Such misunderstandings seem to derive from a lack of contact. McPherson states that "Although he [Ellison] lives in New York and has access to literary and intellectual areas, Ellison seems to have very limited contact with the black writers who also live there." (p. 46) McPherson also explains that Ellison is interested in young black writers and the young black people in general, but his knowledge "of them is limited to sessions during speaking engagements, letters, and what he hears from the media." (p. 49) In fairness, it should be pointed out that the foregoing statements are in a ocntext that do not imply evasion.

There are other differences that derive from Ellison's particular vision, a few of which may be briefly noted. His vision of the opportunity of the individual to find his freedom through the chaos that hovers about the edges of rituals by which society organizes itself, expressed in his essay "Society, Morality, and the Novel," would not satisfy those who do not feel that the individual really wins thereby a significant victory.[13] The same principle would apply to the implication that the intermeshing of black culture provides either the black individual or the group with a source of ultimate power to change American culture to his advantage, in the normal process of things. Julius Lester in his essay "Race and Revolution" does suggest that black culture has been a considerable resource for young rebel whites, but concludes that each side will probably have to work out its own hangups separately before there can be a coming together.[14] As to Ellison's celebration of the great Western writers as models, some of them would not be denied as a resource for techniques, but resources from the East and Africa would also receive emphasis.

It is clear that there are fundamental issues on which Ellison and some younger writers would have to agree to disagree. But, outside the areas of disagreement, what remains is Ellison's grasp of brilliant resources in techniques essential to the building of an effective black writing tradition, which are the rightful heritage of a younger generation. Perhaps they may be obtained, even if the process is characterized by "antagonistic cooperation."

FOOTNOTES

1. "Recent Negro Fiction," *New Masses* 40 (August 5, 1941), pp. 22-26.
2. "Indivisible Man," *Atlantic Monthly* (December, 1970), p. 50.
3. "Transition," *The Negro Quarterly* I (Spring, 1942), pp. 89-92.
4. A Very Stern Discipline," *Harpers* Magazine (March, 1967), pp. 77-78.
5. *The Souls of Black Folk* (New York, 1951), p. 87.
6. *Wretched of the Earth* (New York, 1966), pp. 85-118, 252-255.
7. *Ibid.*, p. 254.
8. "A Very Stern Discipline," p. 88.
9. "Indivisible Man," p. 47.
10. *Ibid.*, p. 55.
11. *Negro Digest* (January, 1968), p. 6.
12. *Ibid.*, pp. 35, 181-184.
13. Granville Hicks, *The Living Novel* (New York, 1962), pp. 65-97.
14. Mel Watkins, ed., *Black Review #1*, pp. 68-86.

Index

DISCARD